Geometic Patterns
Coloring Book
45 Designs - Beginner to Advanced

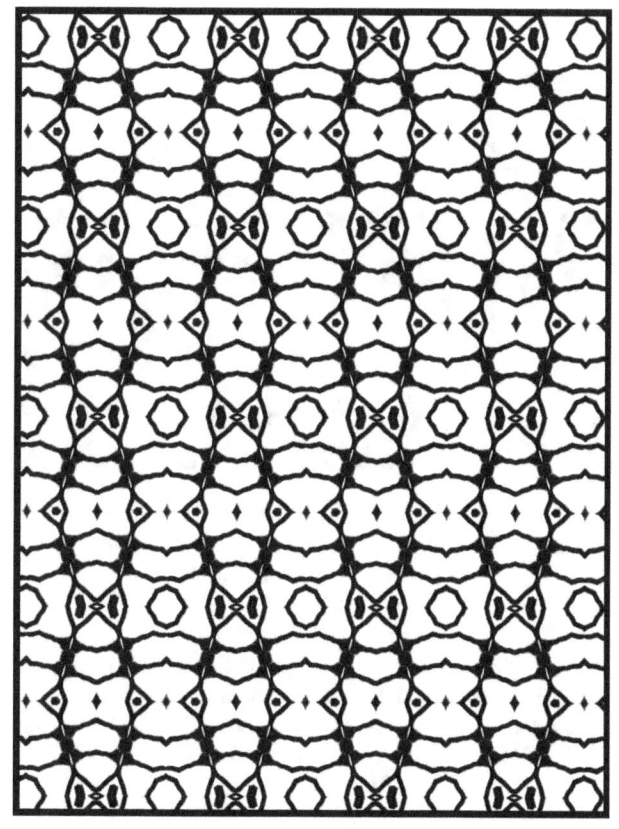

Adult Coloring Book
GRACE BRANNIGAN

Design Elaine Warfield

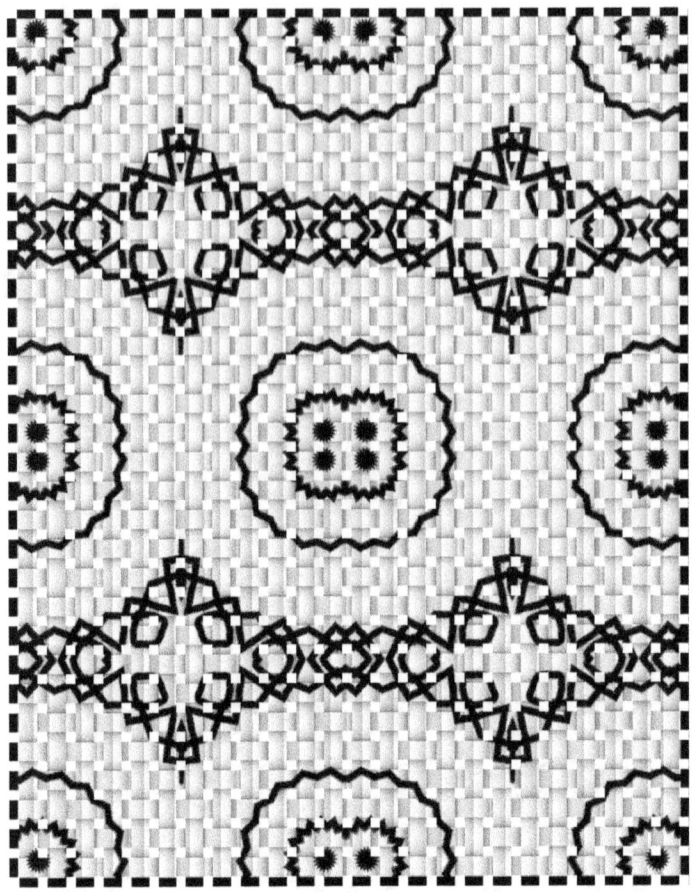

Author Website: http://www.ColoringBooksForAdults.info
Geometric Patterns Coloring Book: 45 Designs Beginner to Advanced
Copyright 2016 Elaine Warfield
ISBN-13: 978-1523908714
ISBN-10: 1523908718
Please check out my other coloring books:
Detailed Mandala Coloring Books 1 through 4
Detailed Alphabet and Renaissance Masks Coloring Books: 25 Grayscale Images
Pocket Size Coloring Books for On-the-Go
Be My Valentine
Vintage Christmas Postcards Vol. 1, 2 and 3
Fairies in the Garden
Scenic Catskill Mountains: 25 Photographs to Color
License Notes

Questor Books, P.O. Box 100, East Jewett, New York, 12424 USA

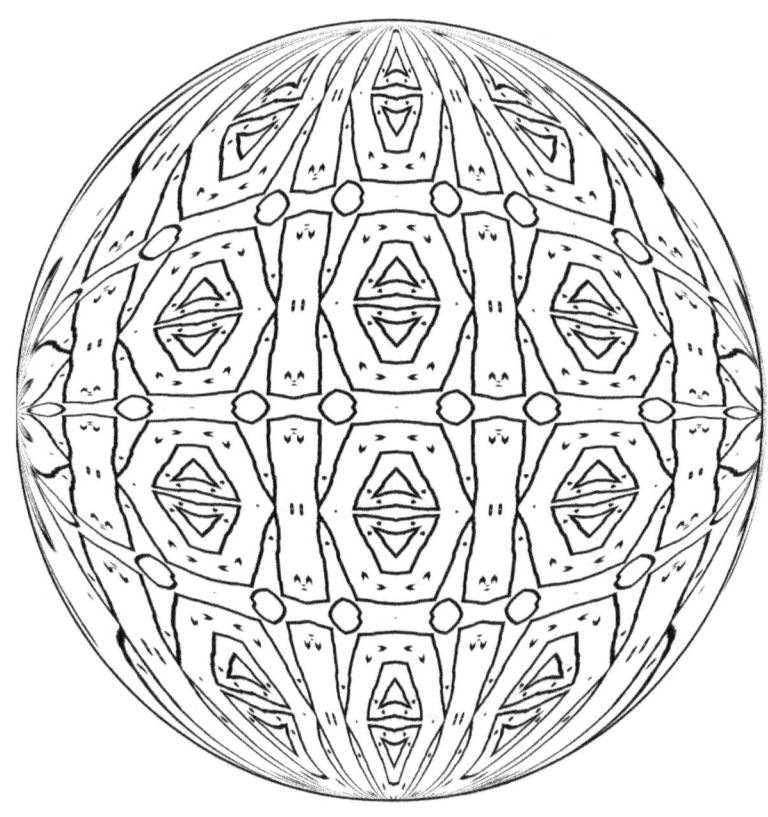

Meditation for your brain -- allow coloring to soothe you.

This coloring book has 45 unique geometric designs and patterns to color. The images are a mix of skill level, and are suitable for beginner colorists to advanced colorists.

∞ ∞ ∞ ∞ ∞ ∞ ∞ ∞ ∞ ∞ ∞ ∞ ∞ ∞ ∞ ∞ ∞

Coloring geometric designs is a unique and fun way to explore color choices and relax at the same time. The end result is a rewarding colored image.

Coloring has been shown to reduce stress and offer meditative release. Create your own visually appealing art using crayons, colored pencils, felt tip markers, ink pens, art pencils, gel pens, glitter pens. There is no limit to your creativity and genius.

Please leave a review where you bought this coloring book and share your coloring images. It really helps the author and other buyers. Please check out my other coloring books and visit my website: **www.ColoringBooksForAdults.Info.**

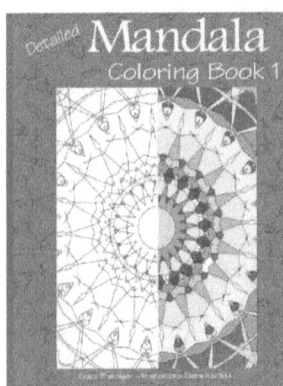
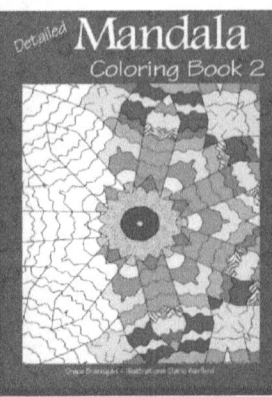
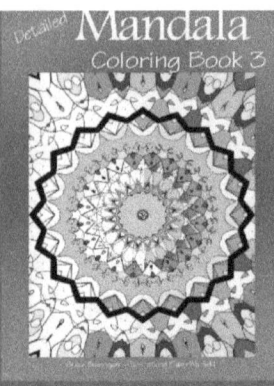
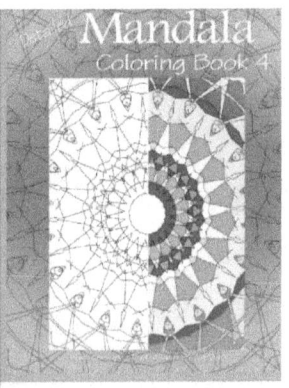

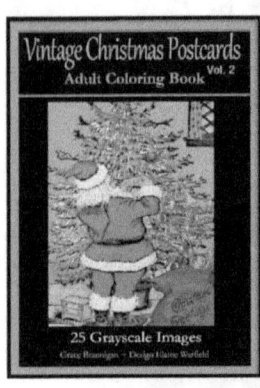
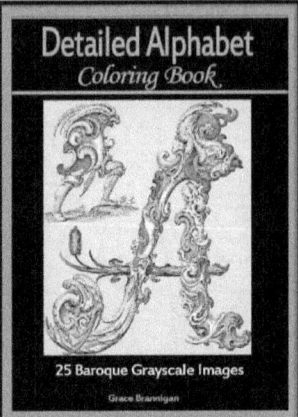
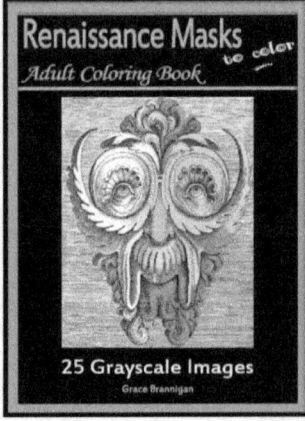
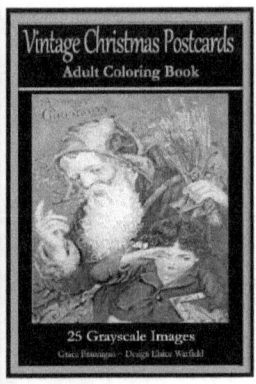

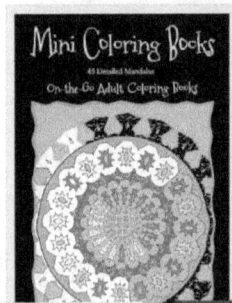
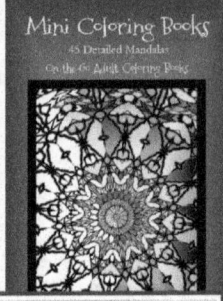
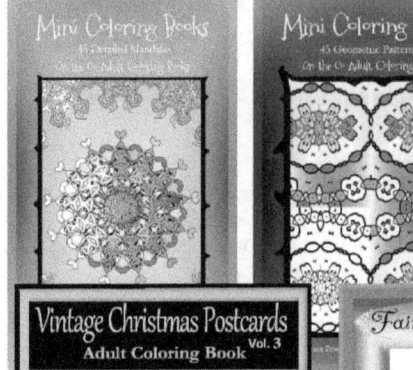

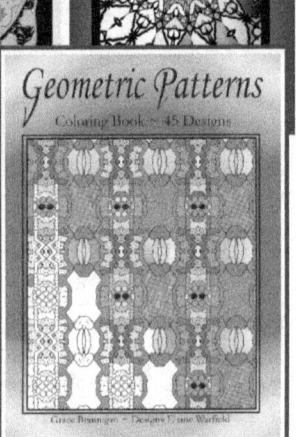
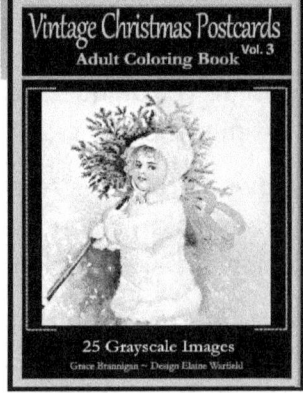
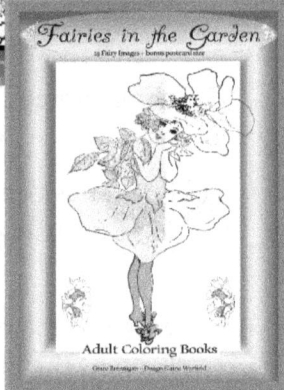

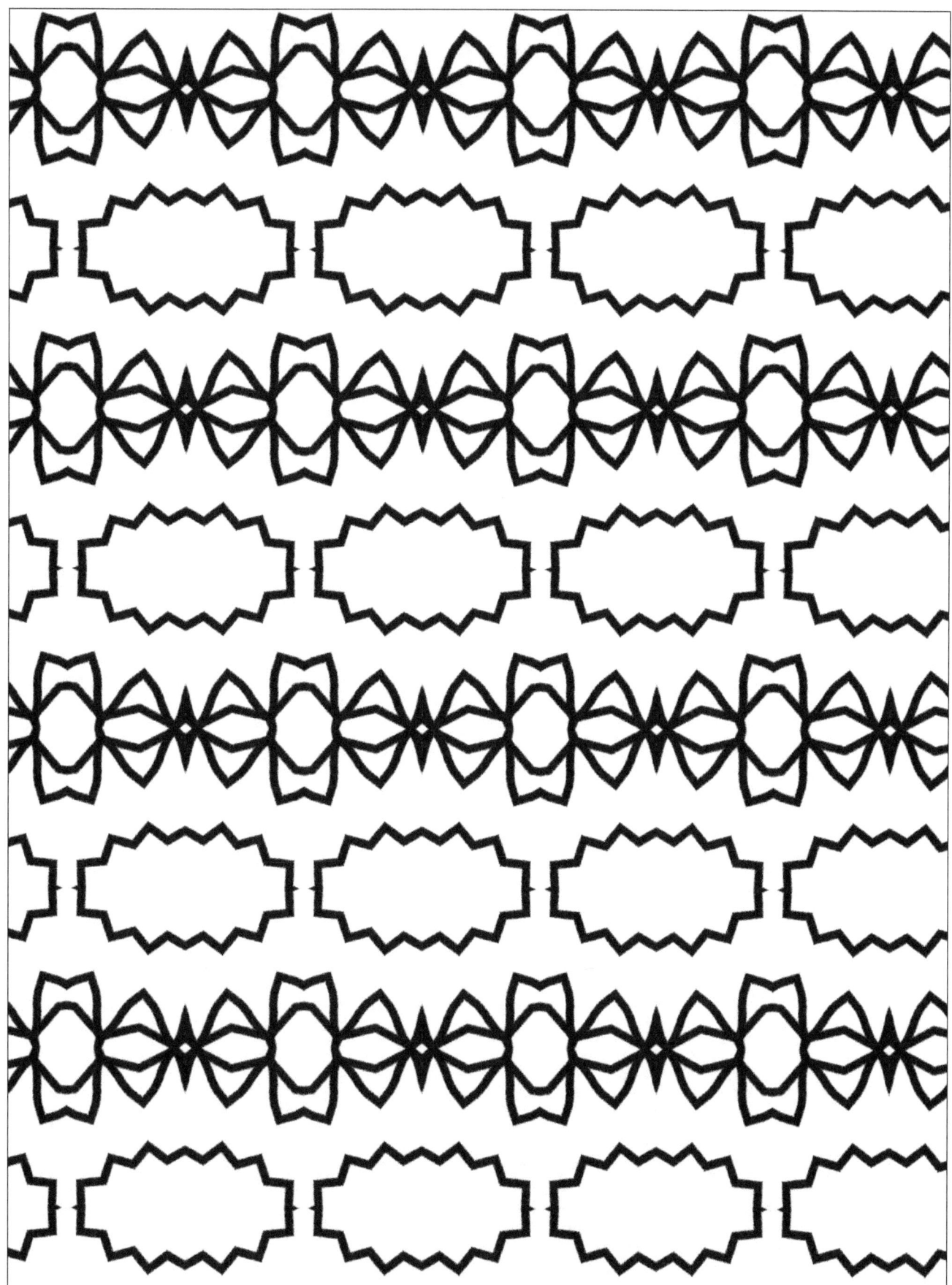

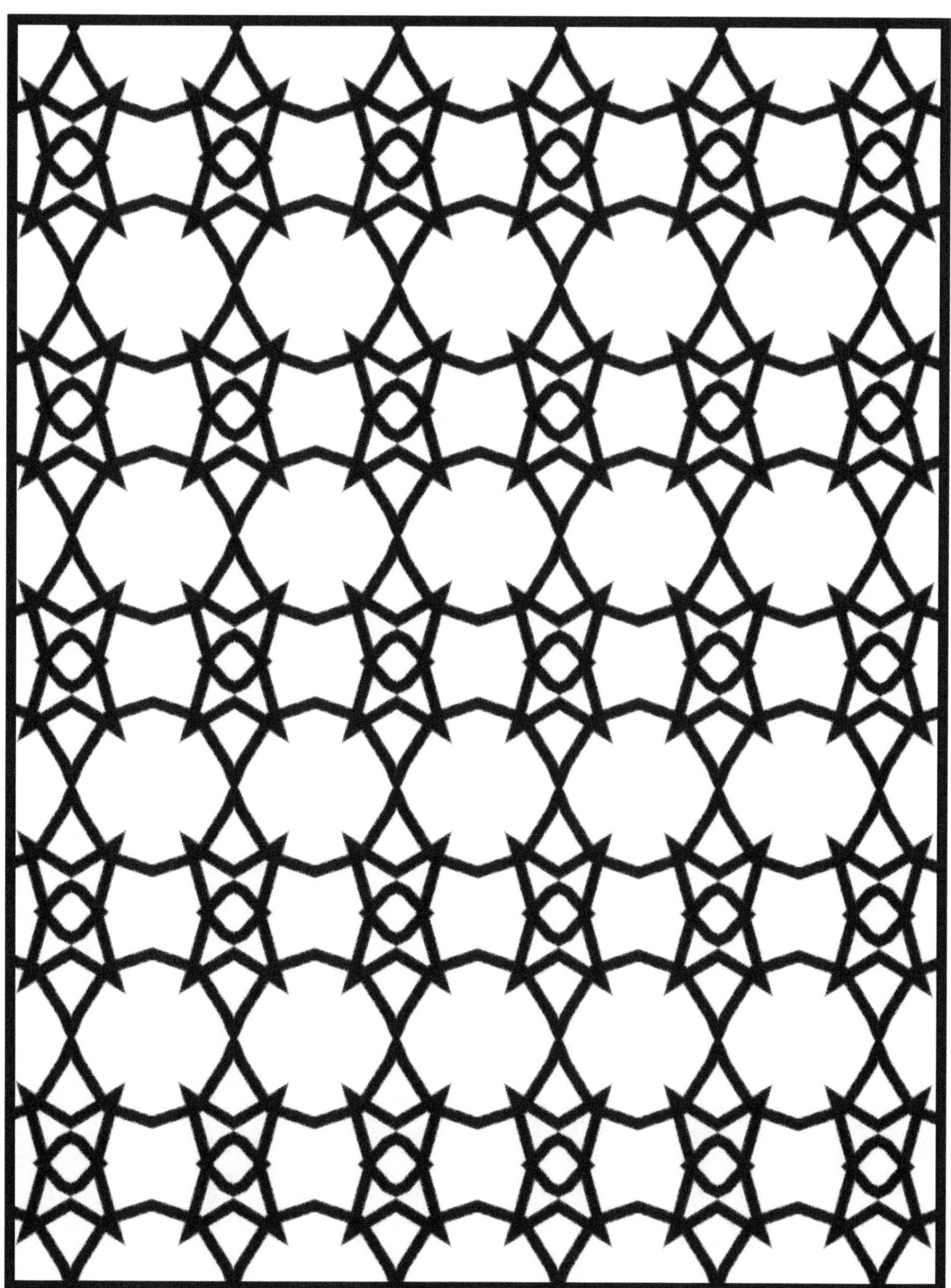

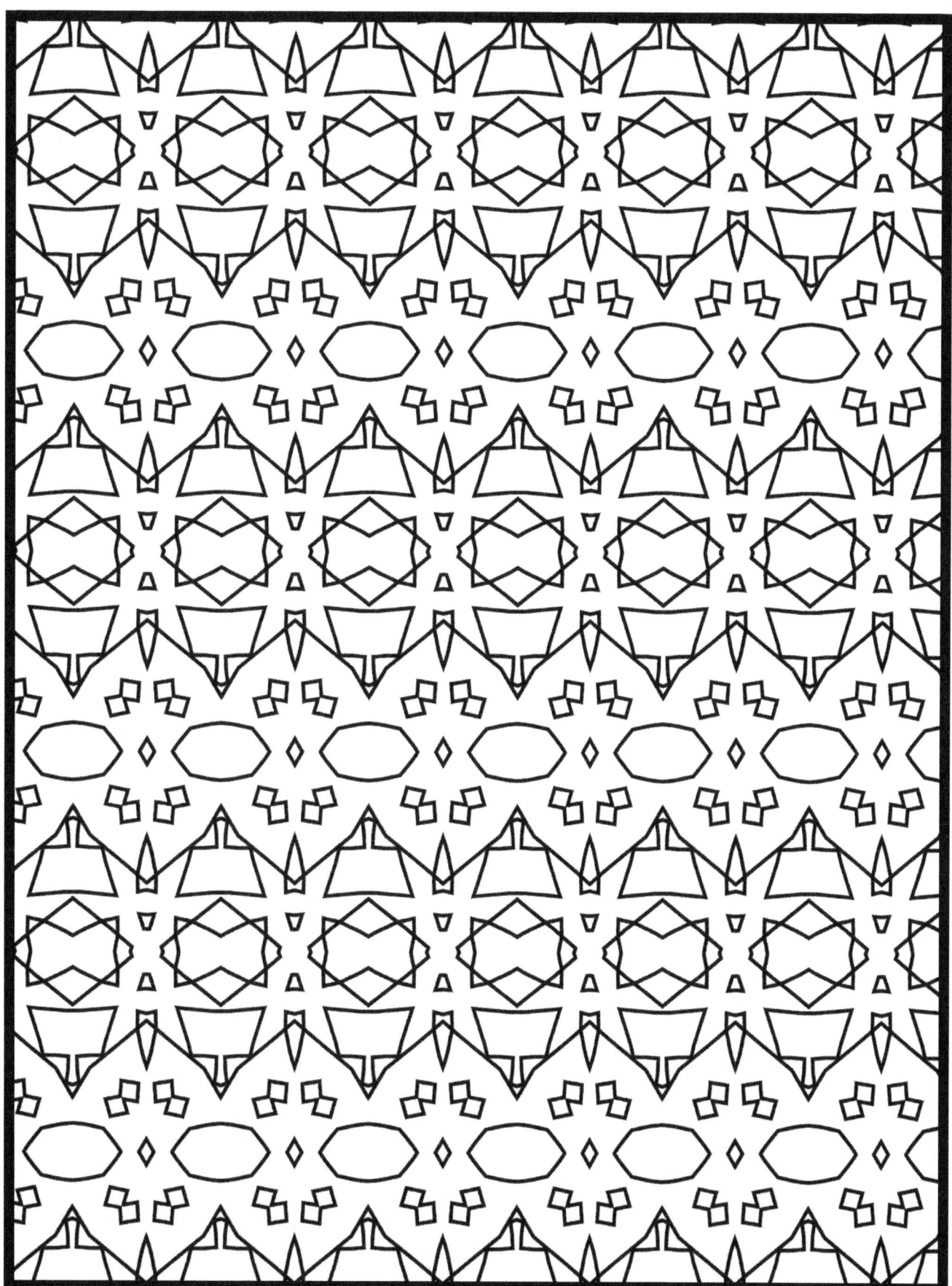

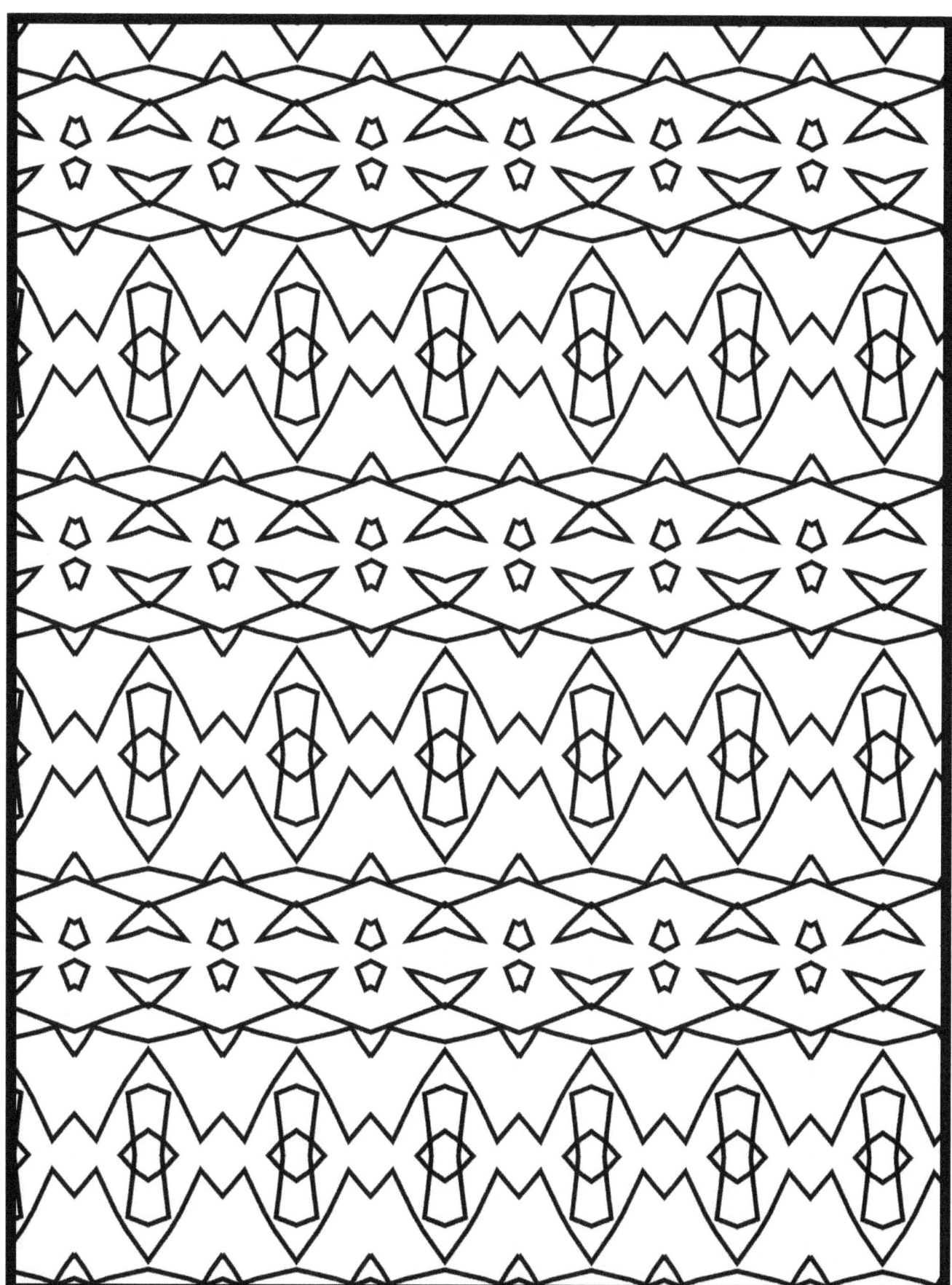

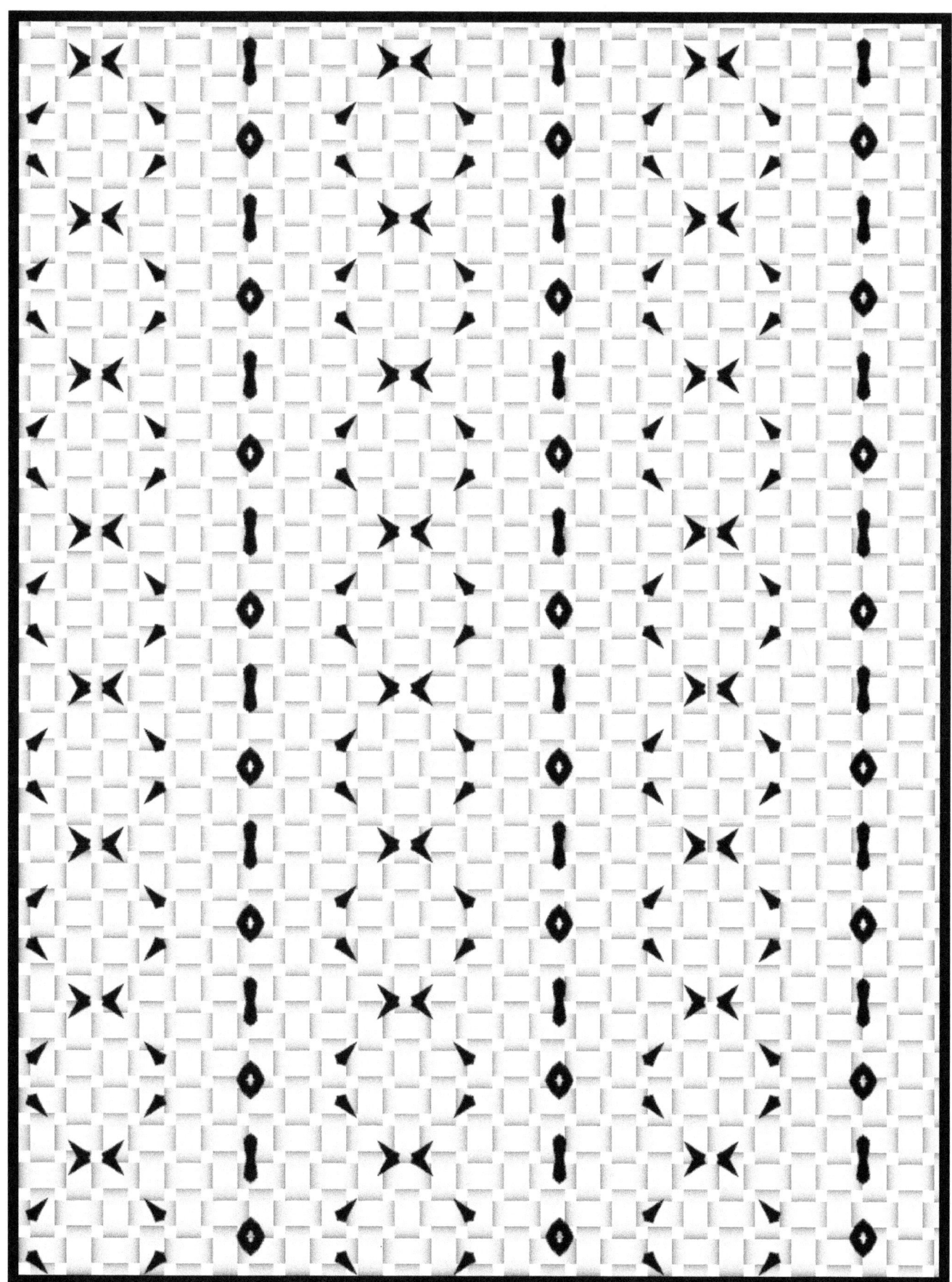

13

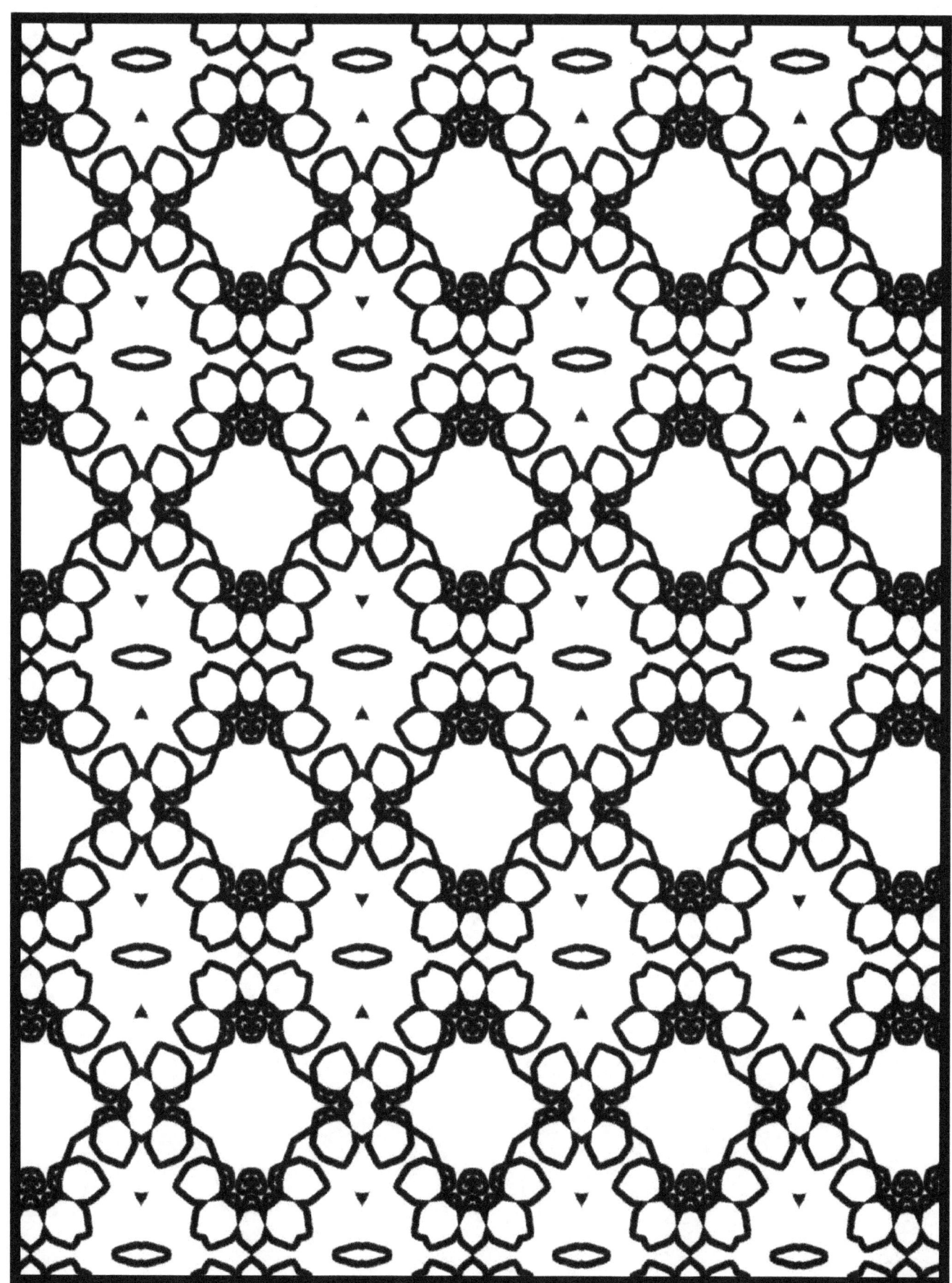

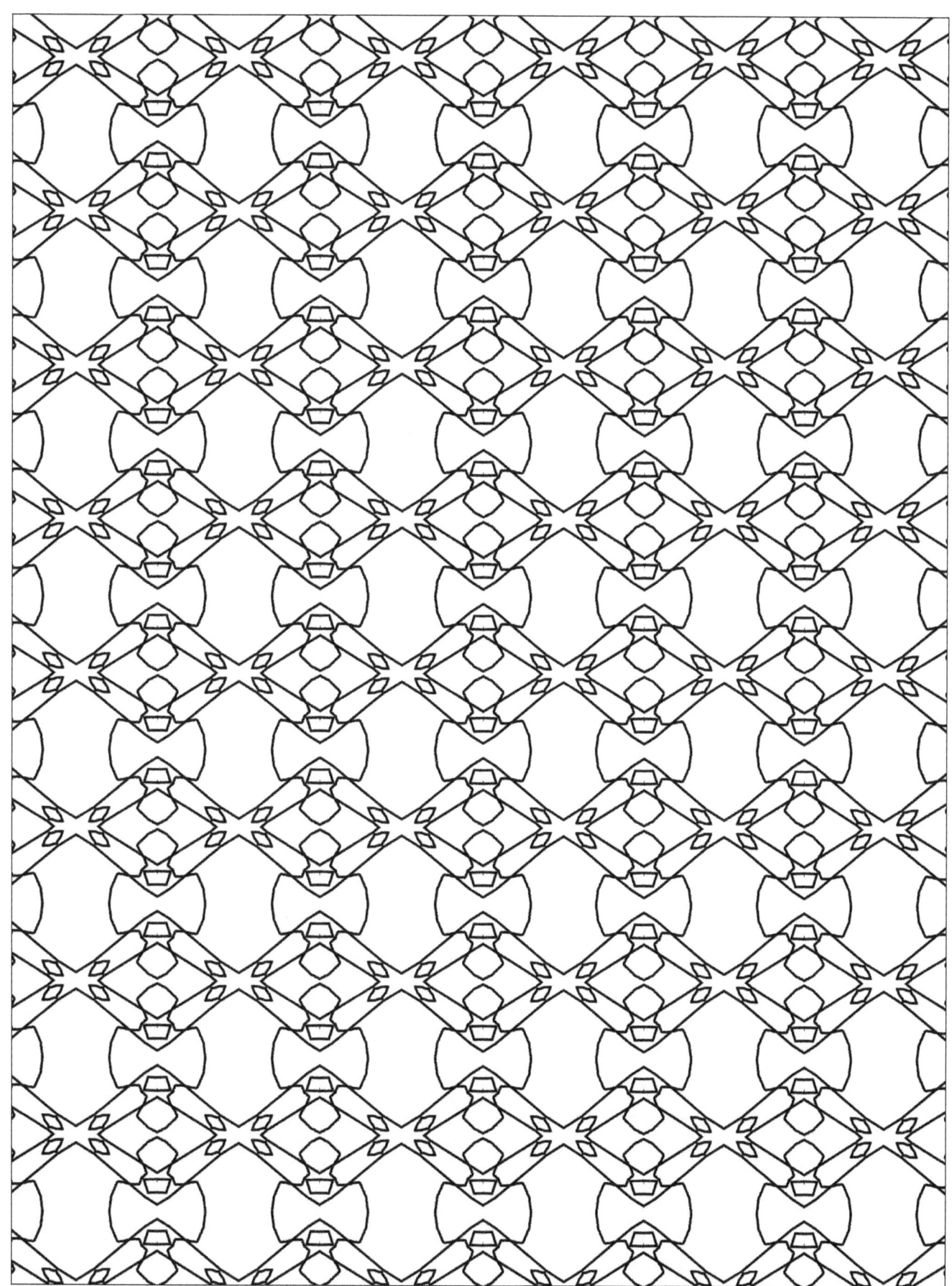

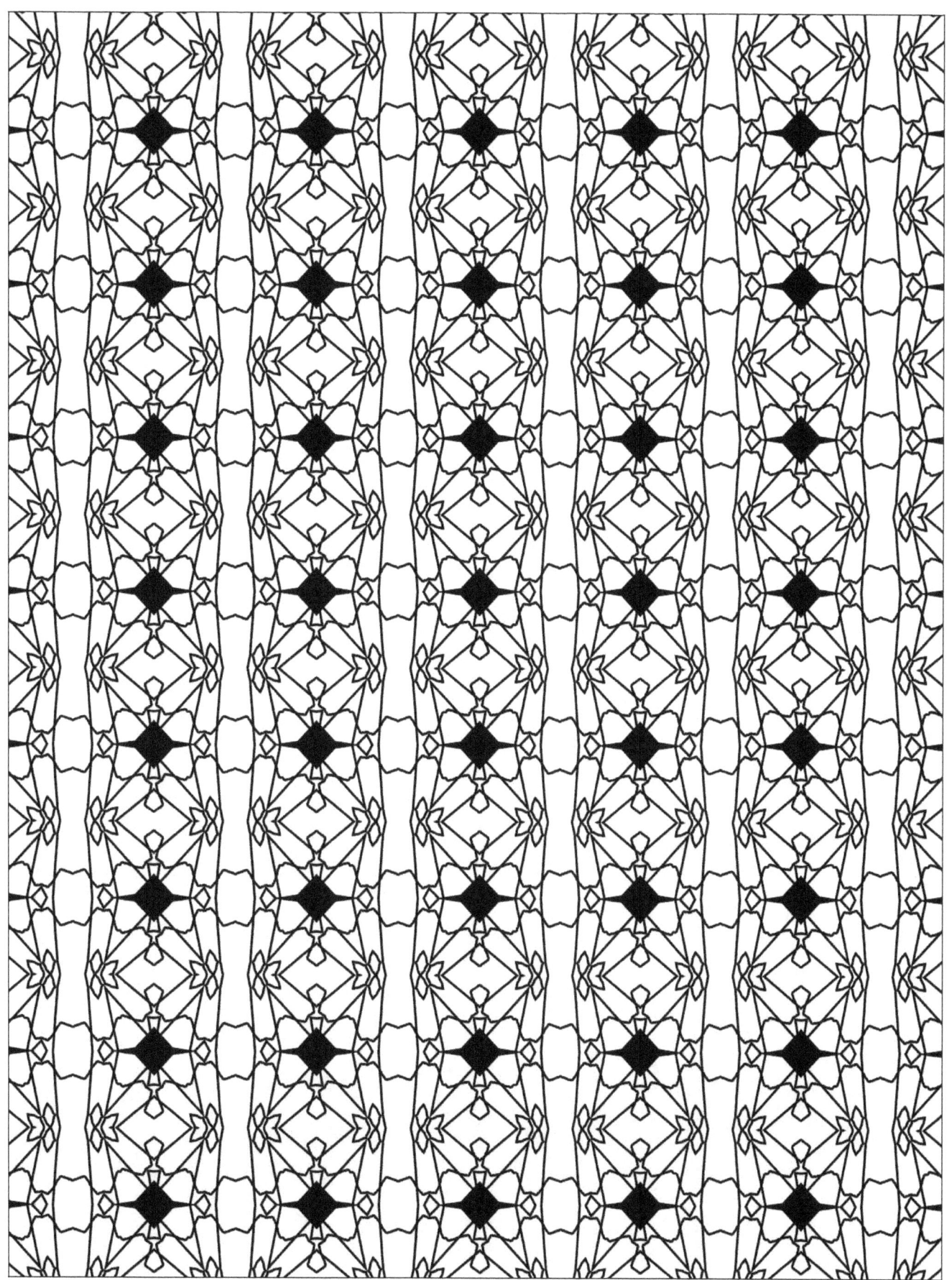

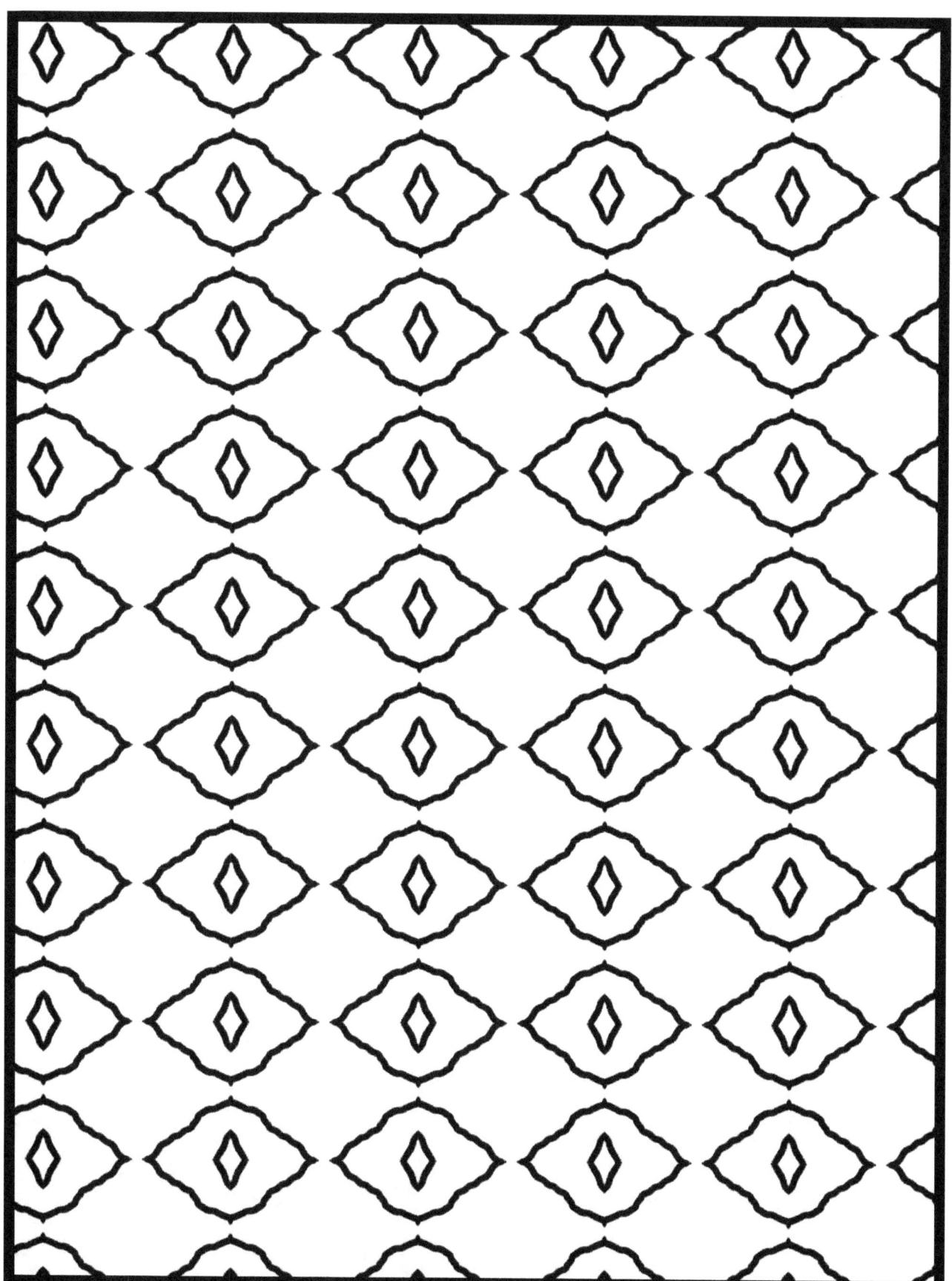

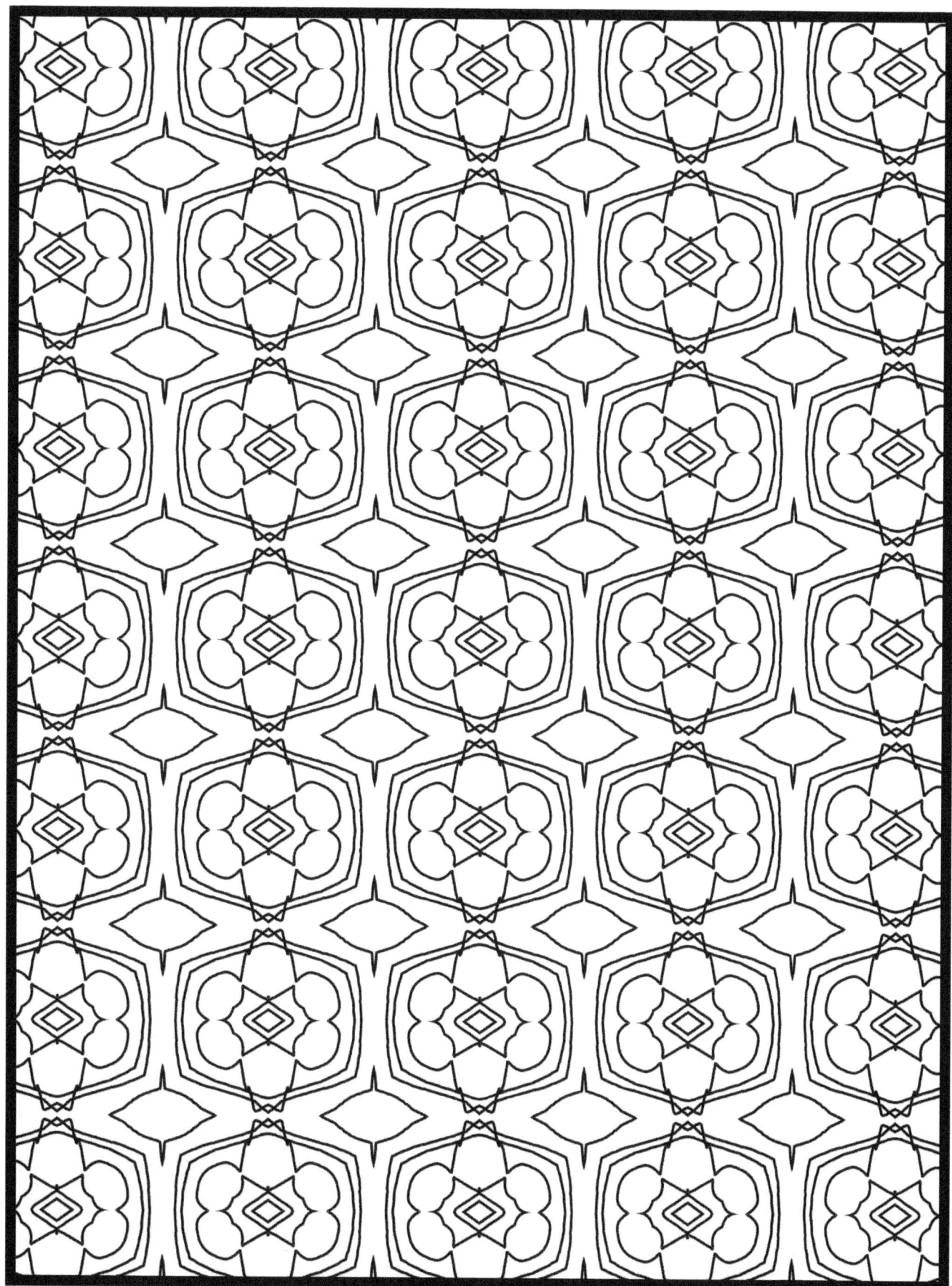

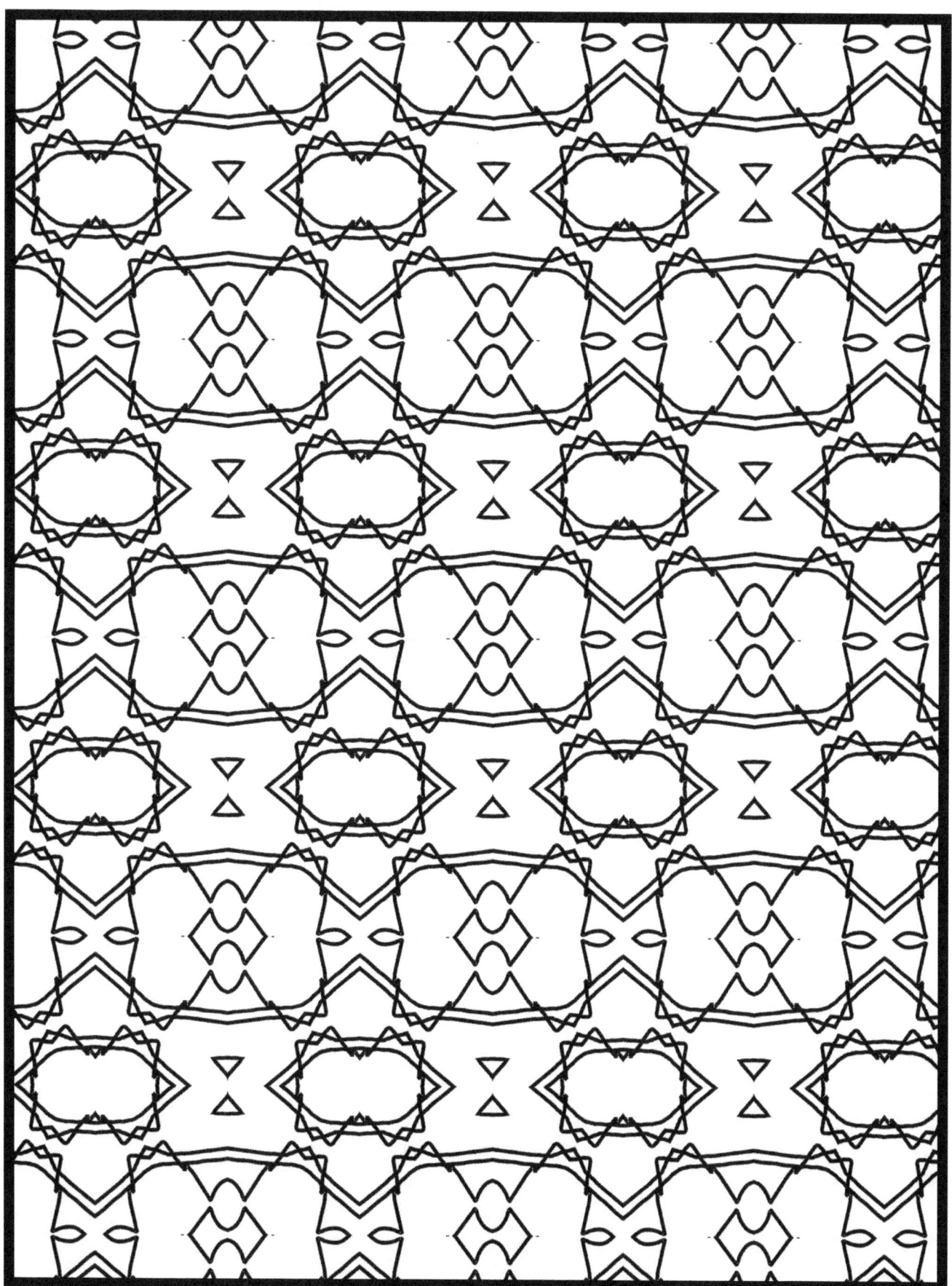

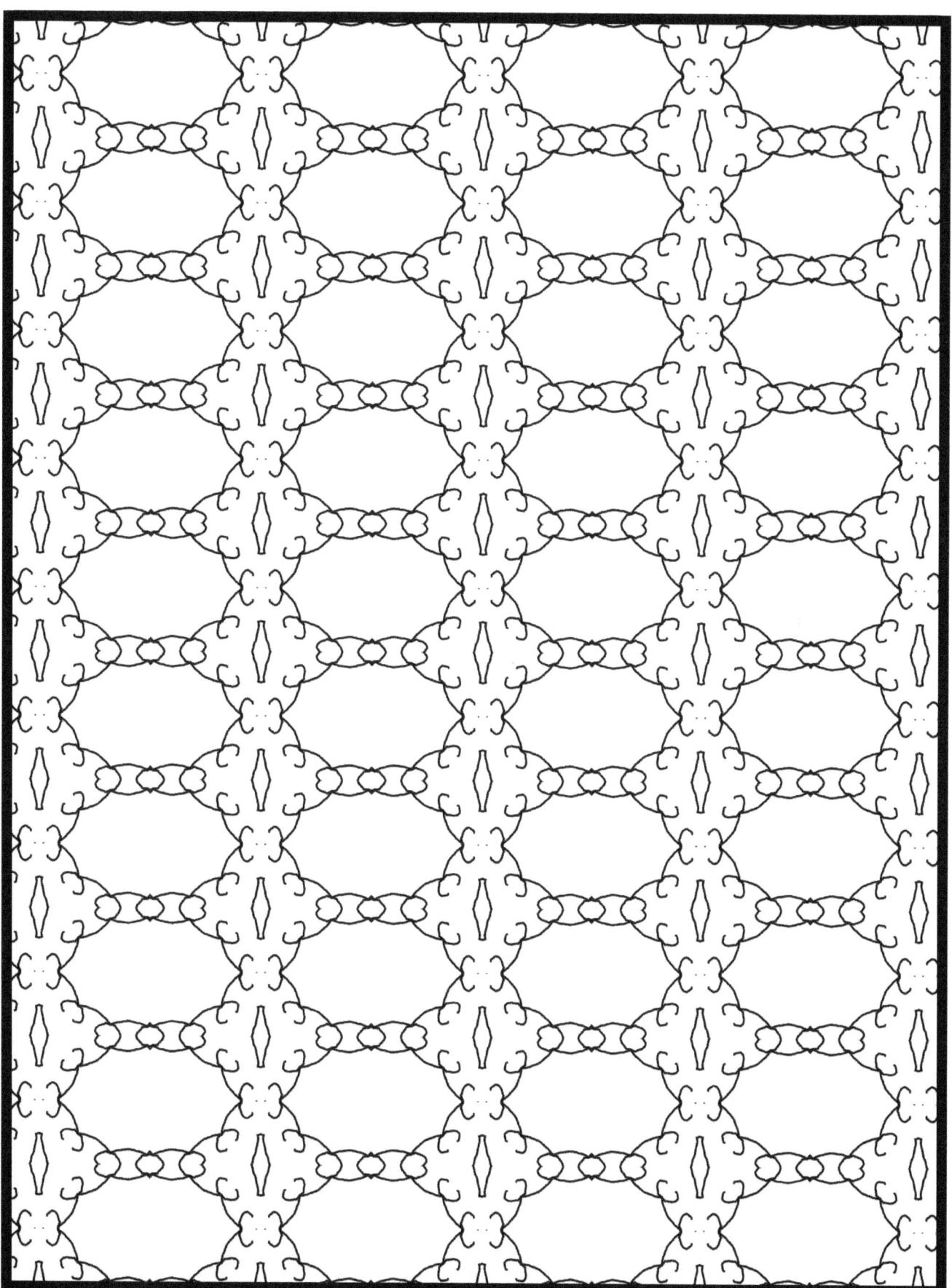

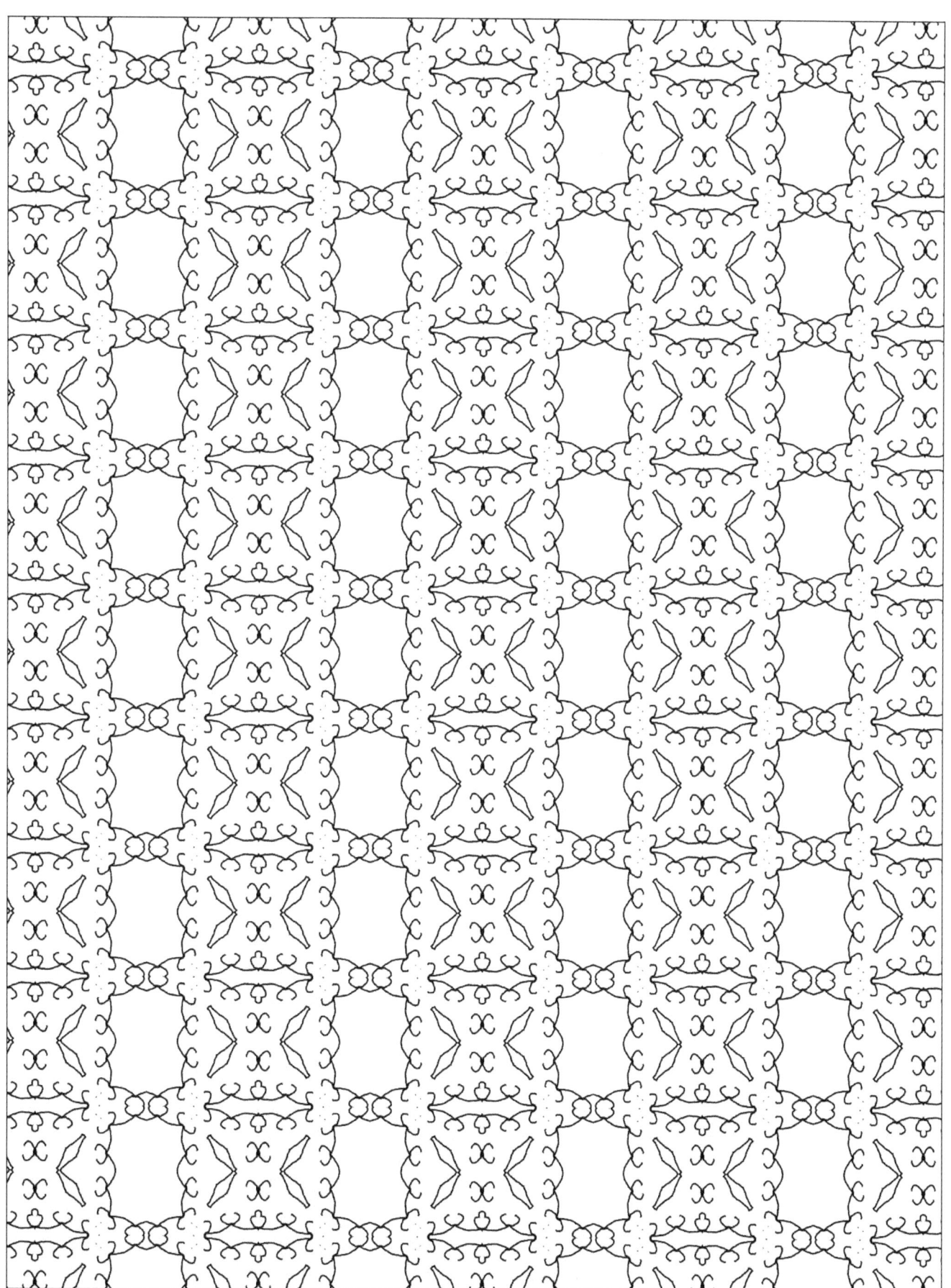

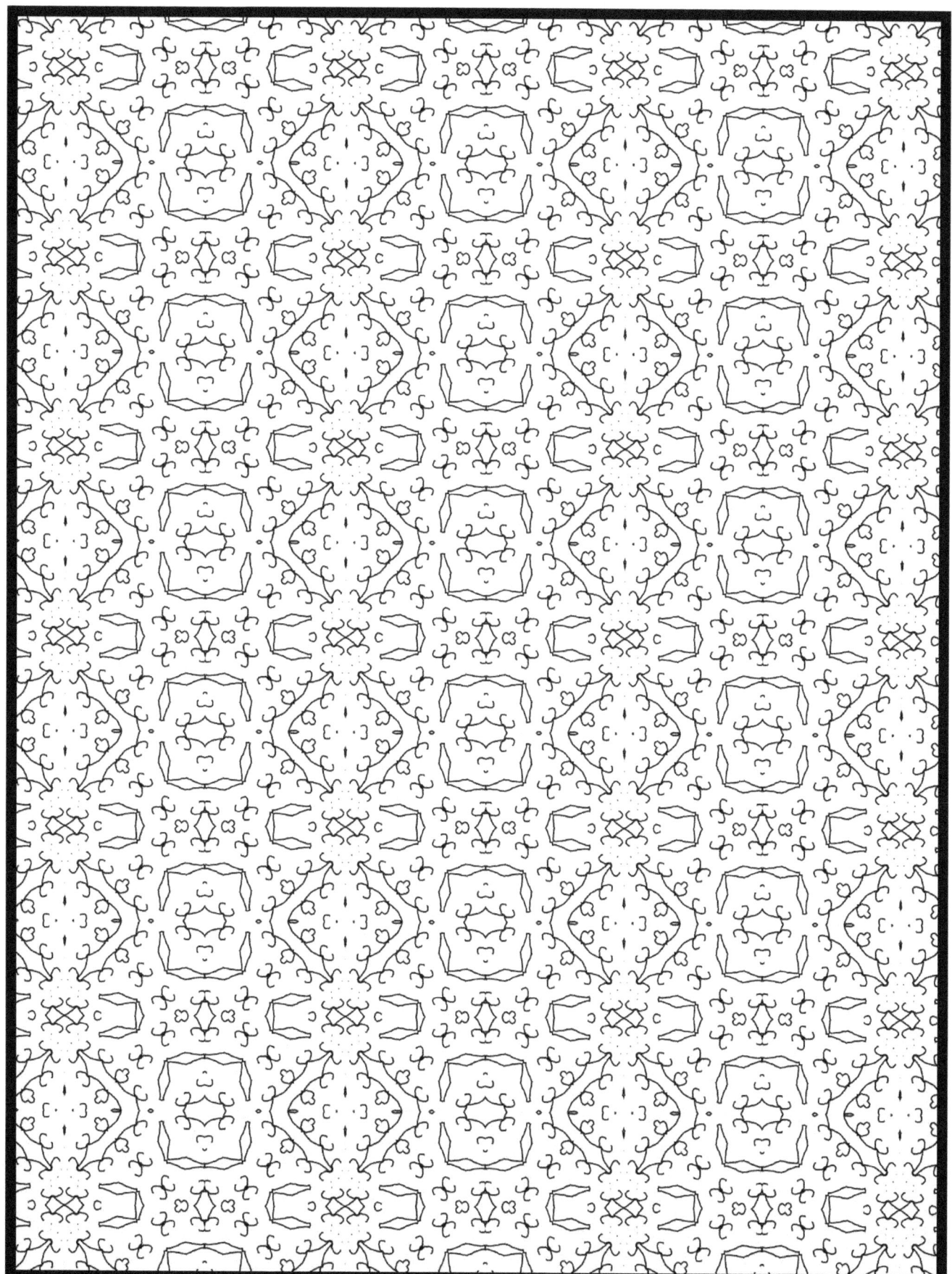

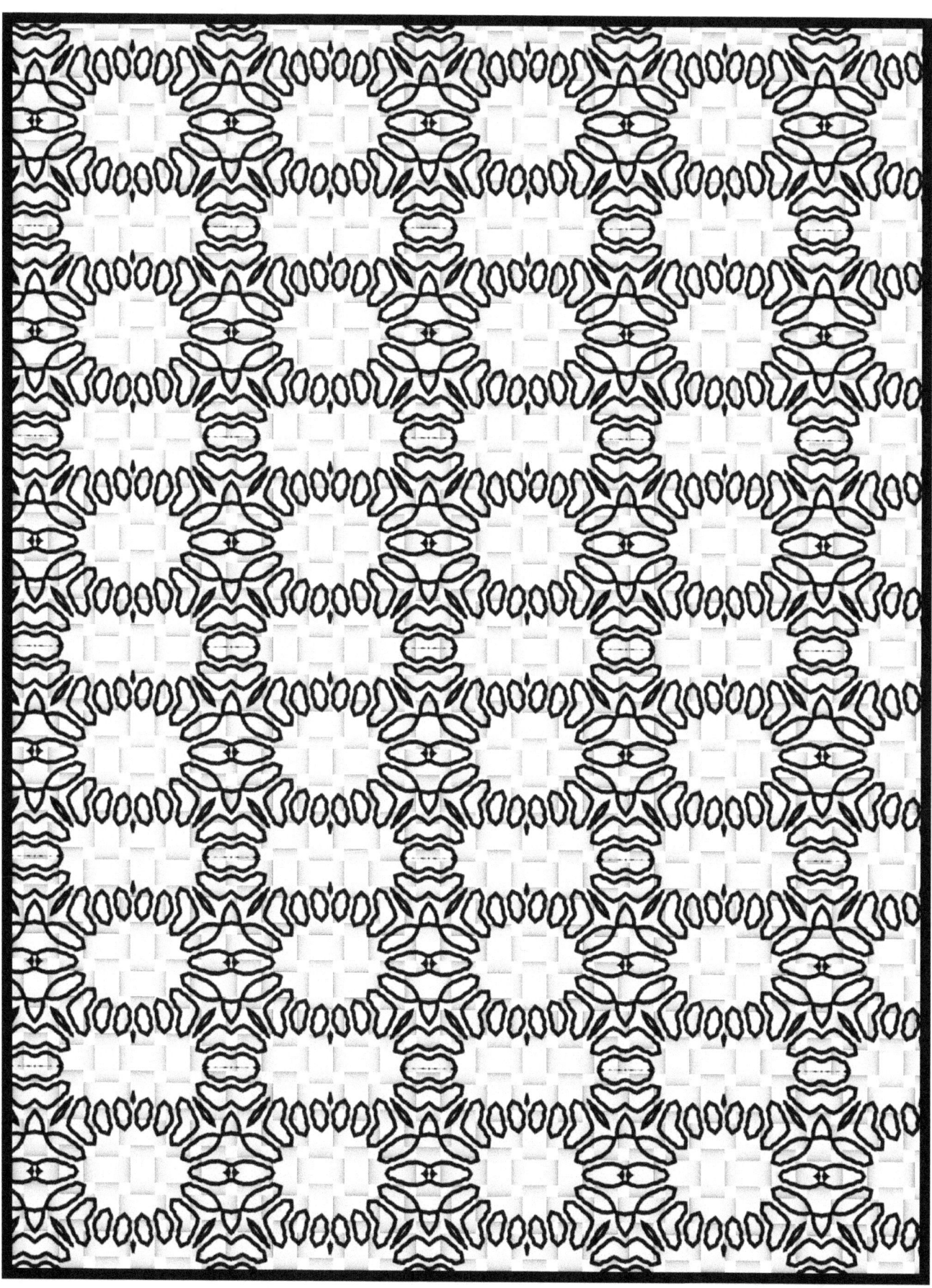

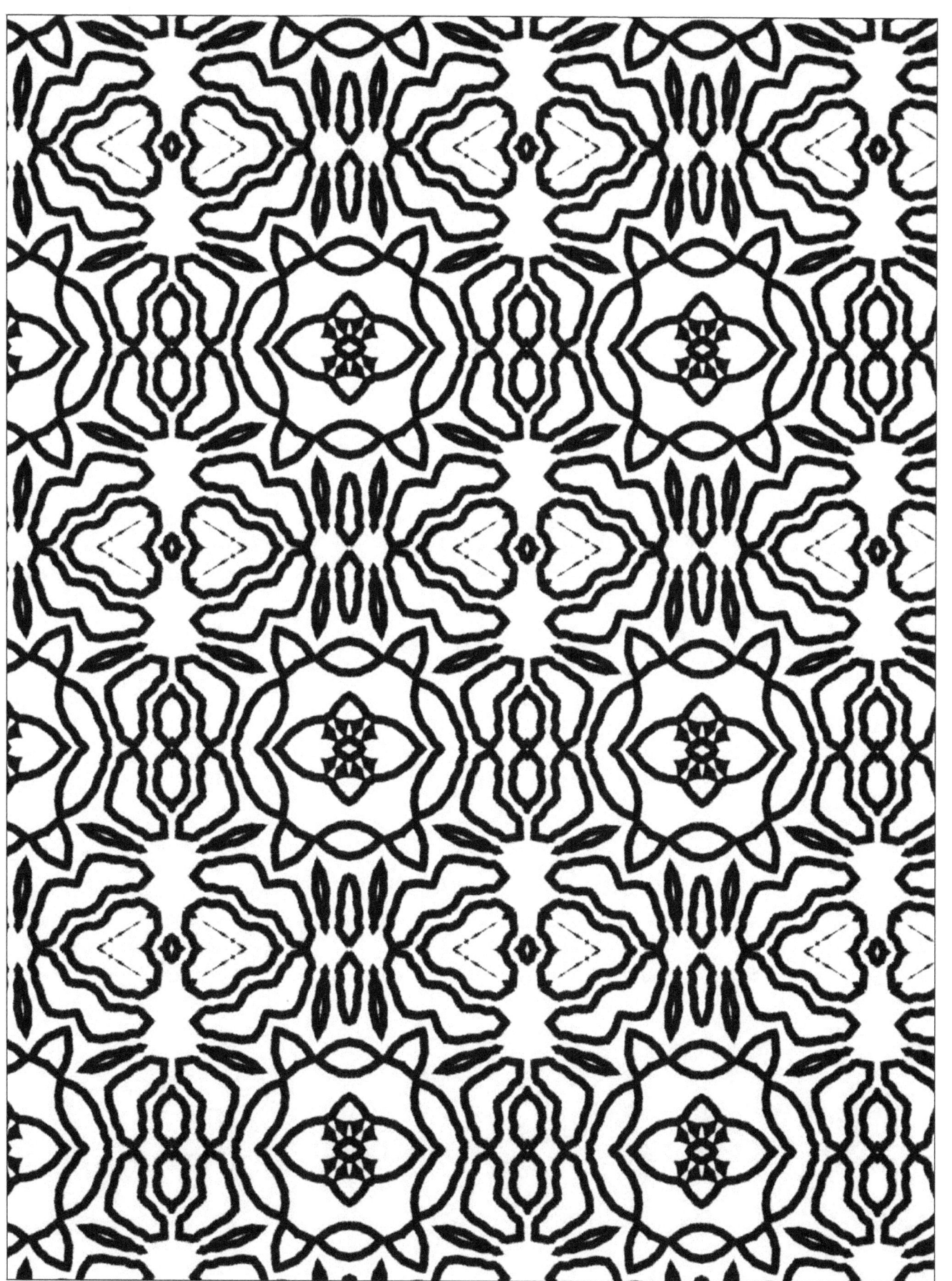

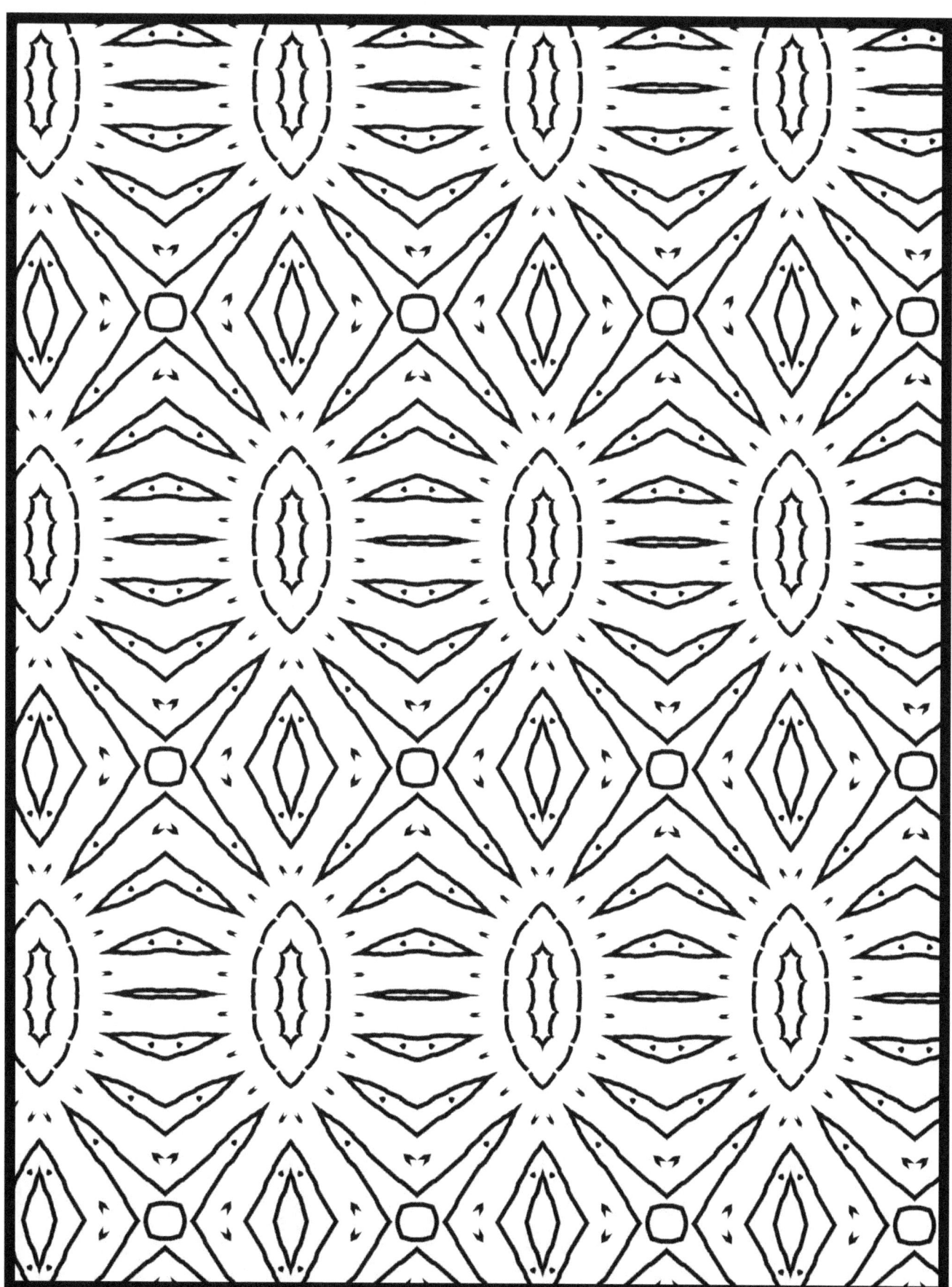

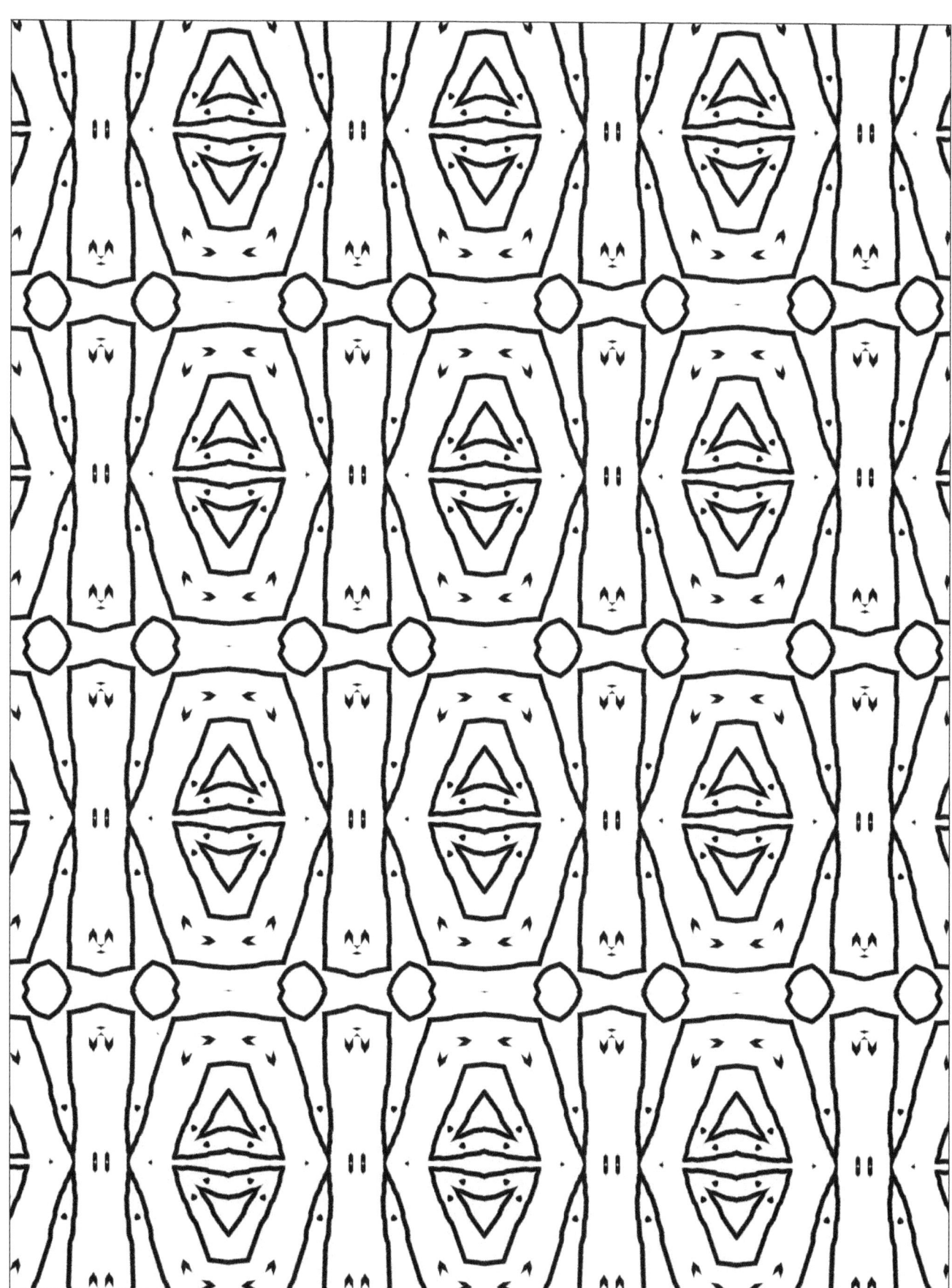

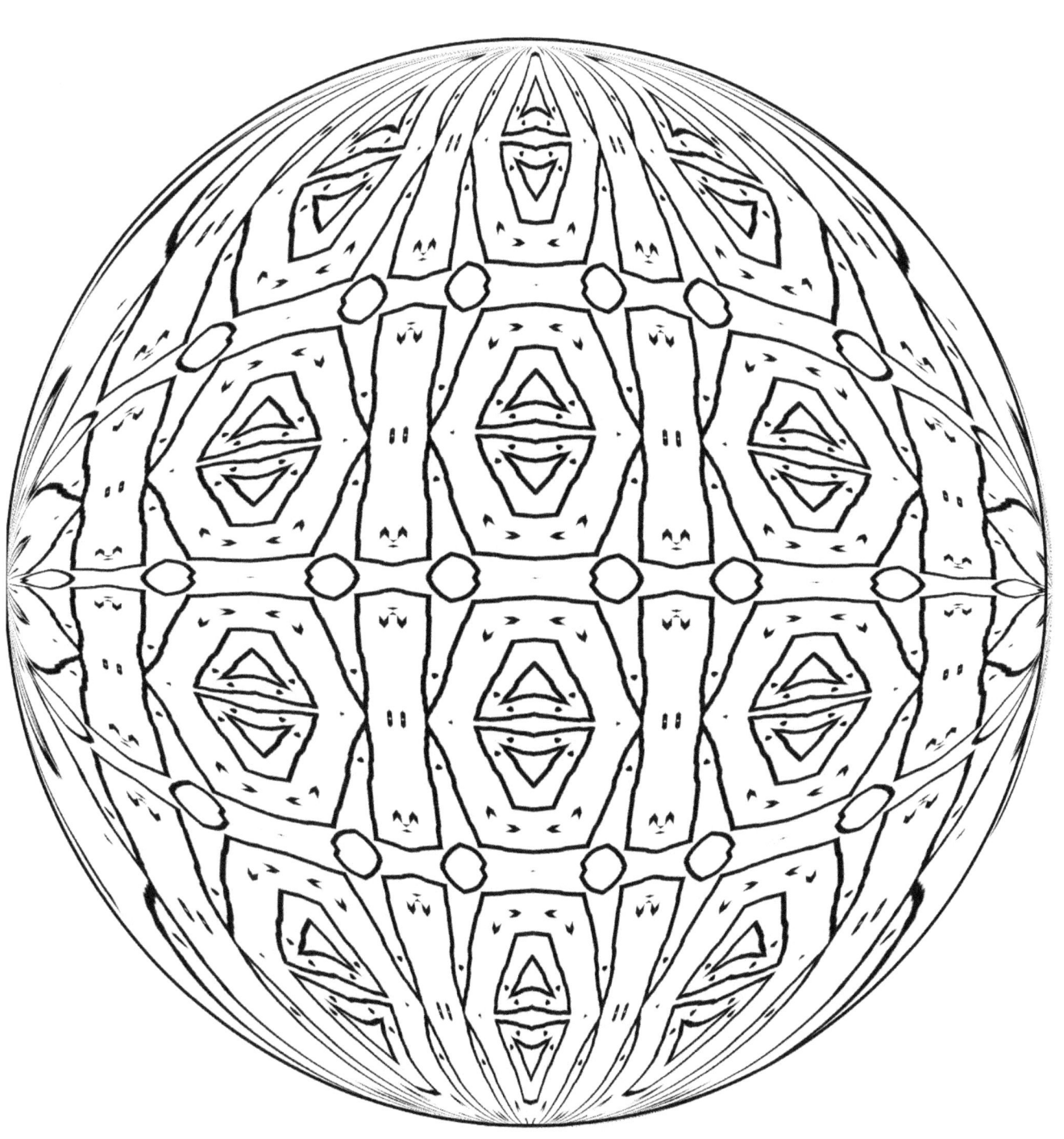

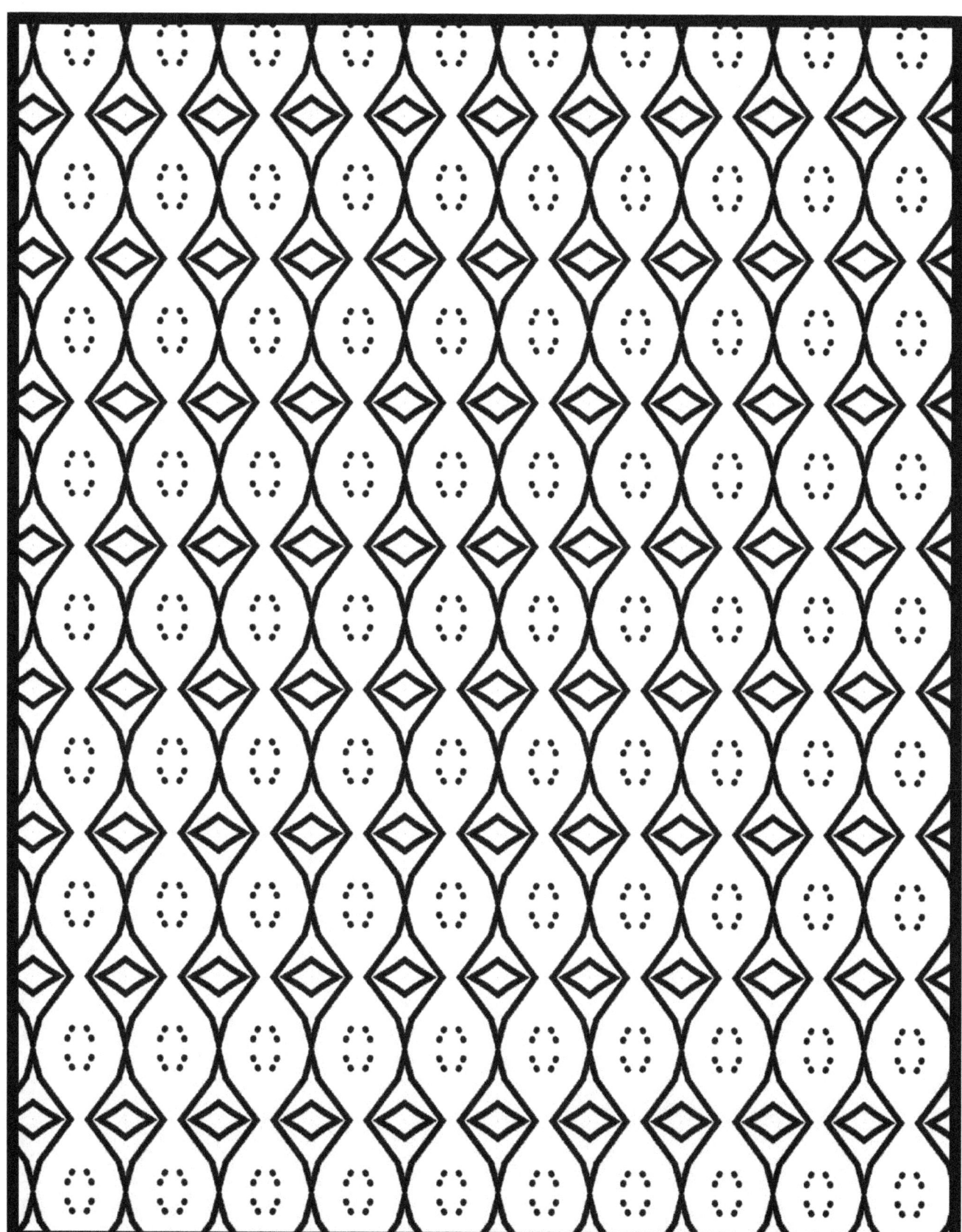

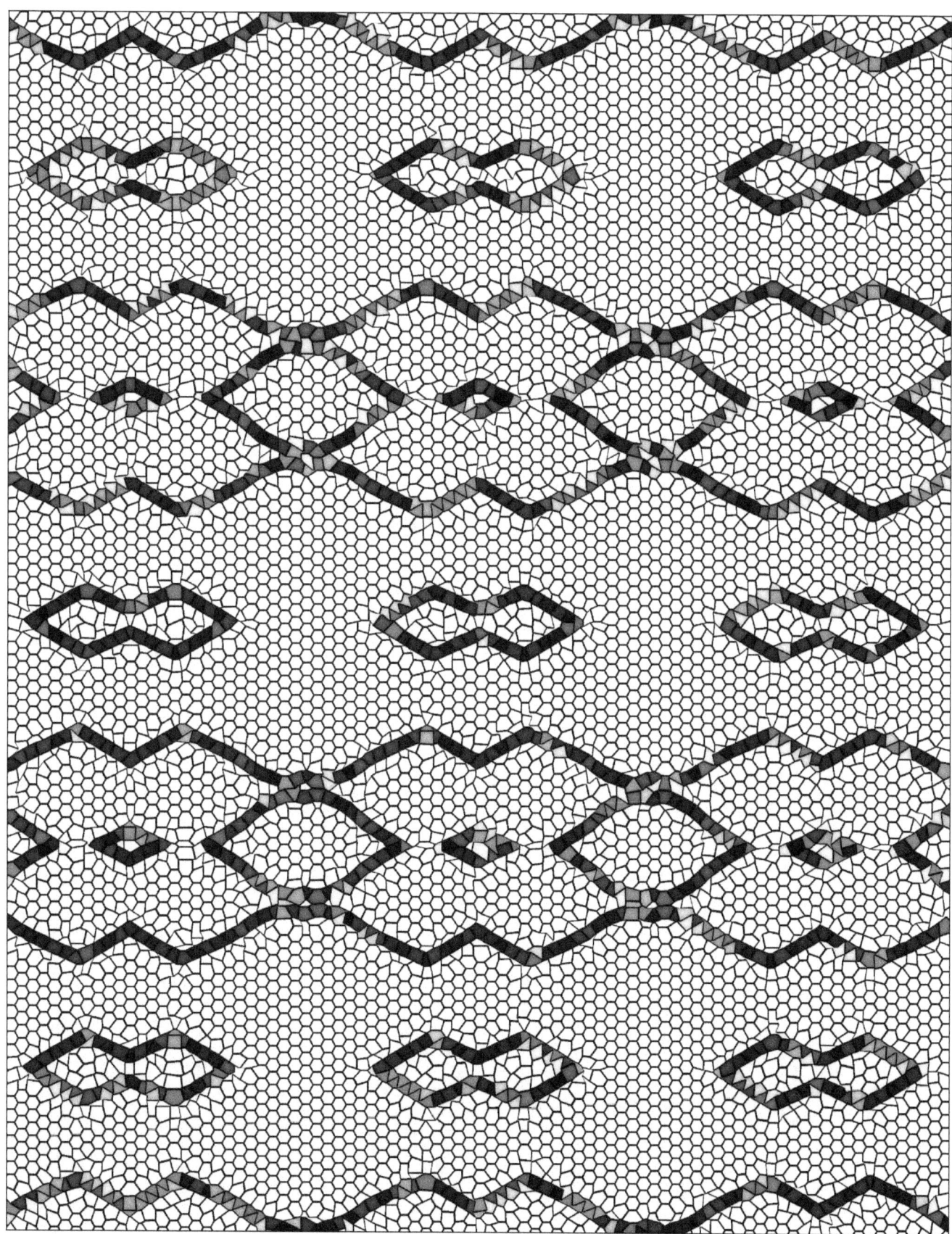

45

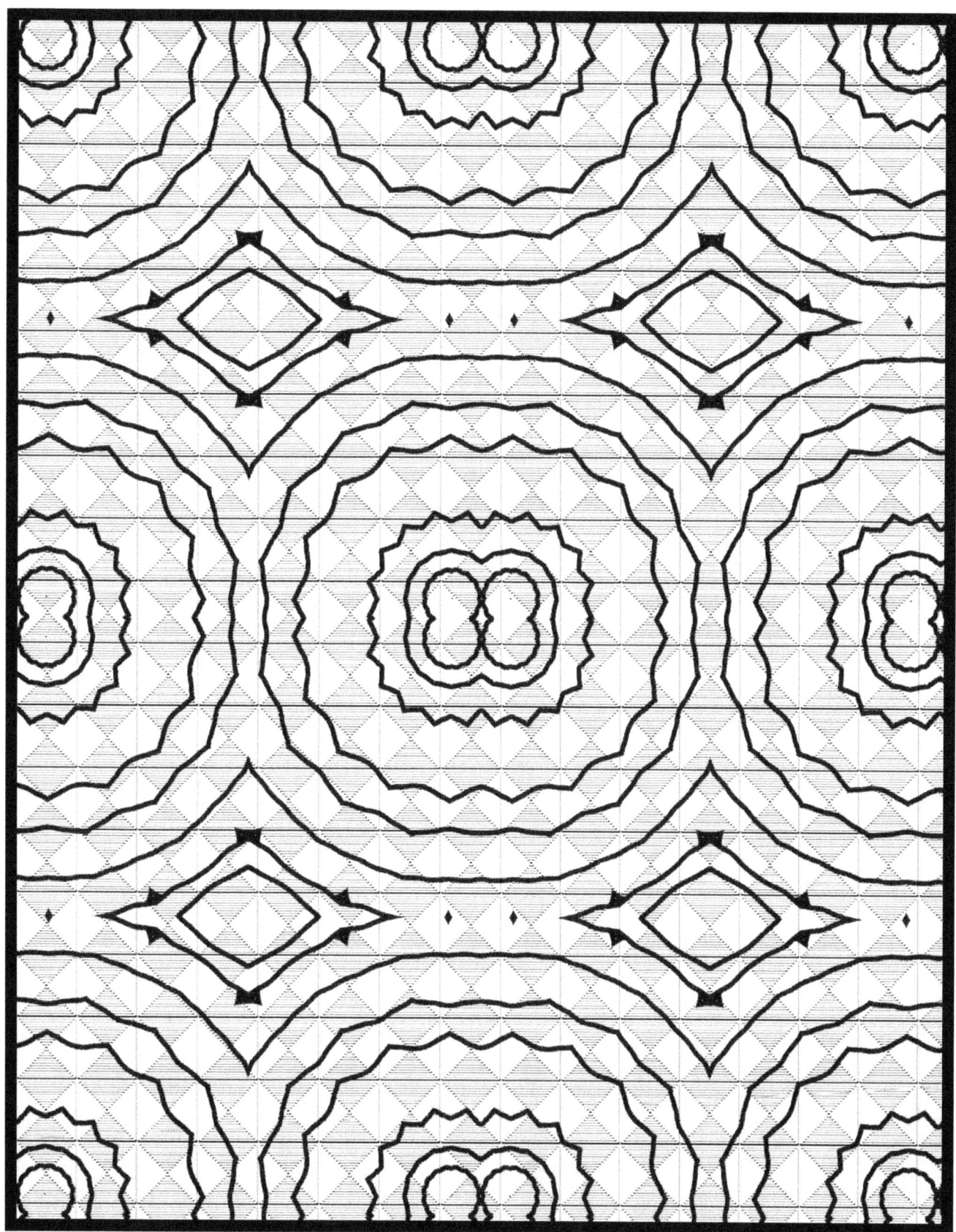

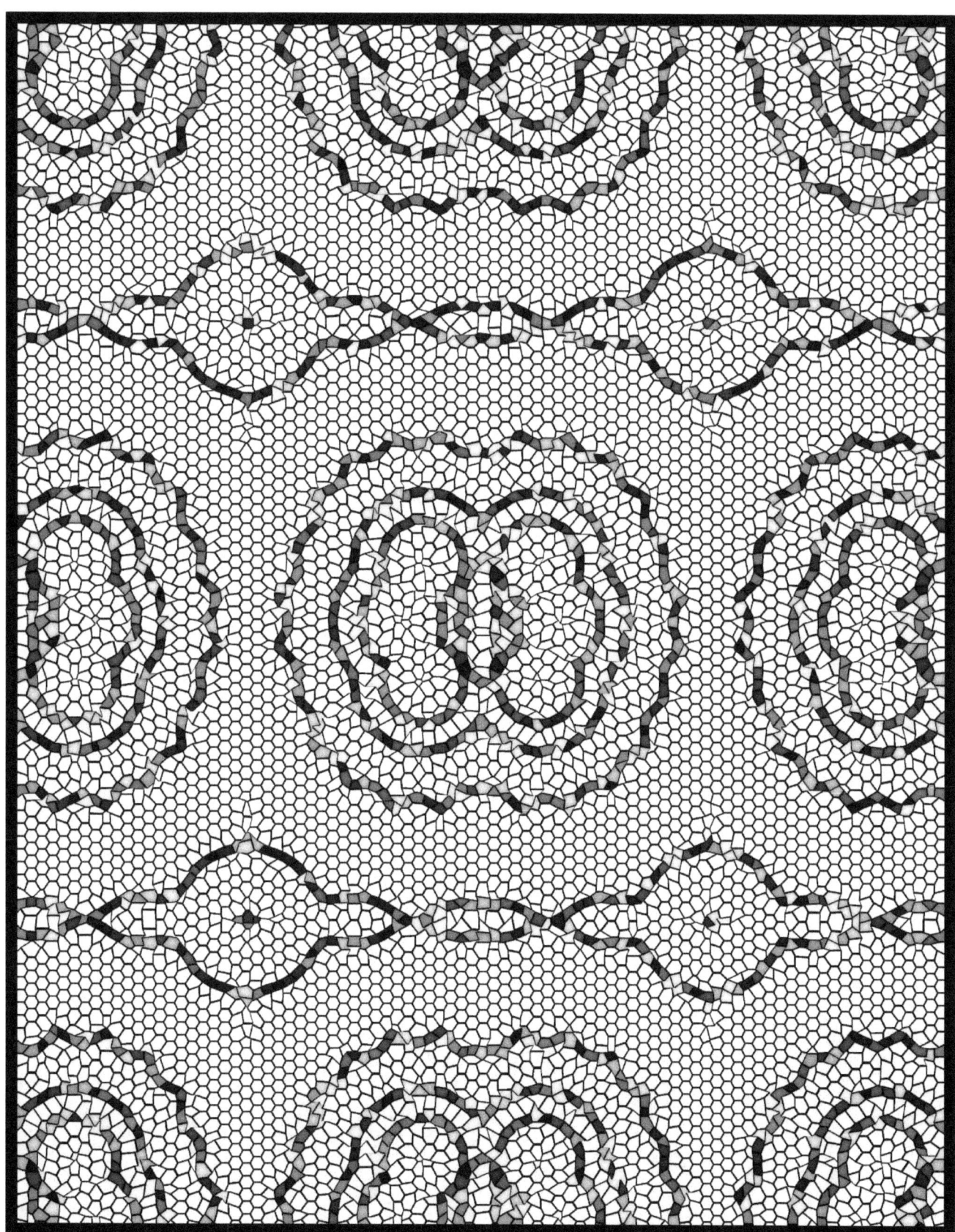

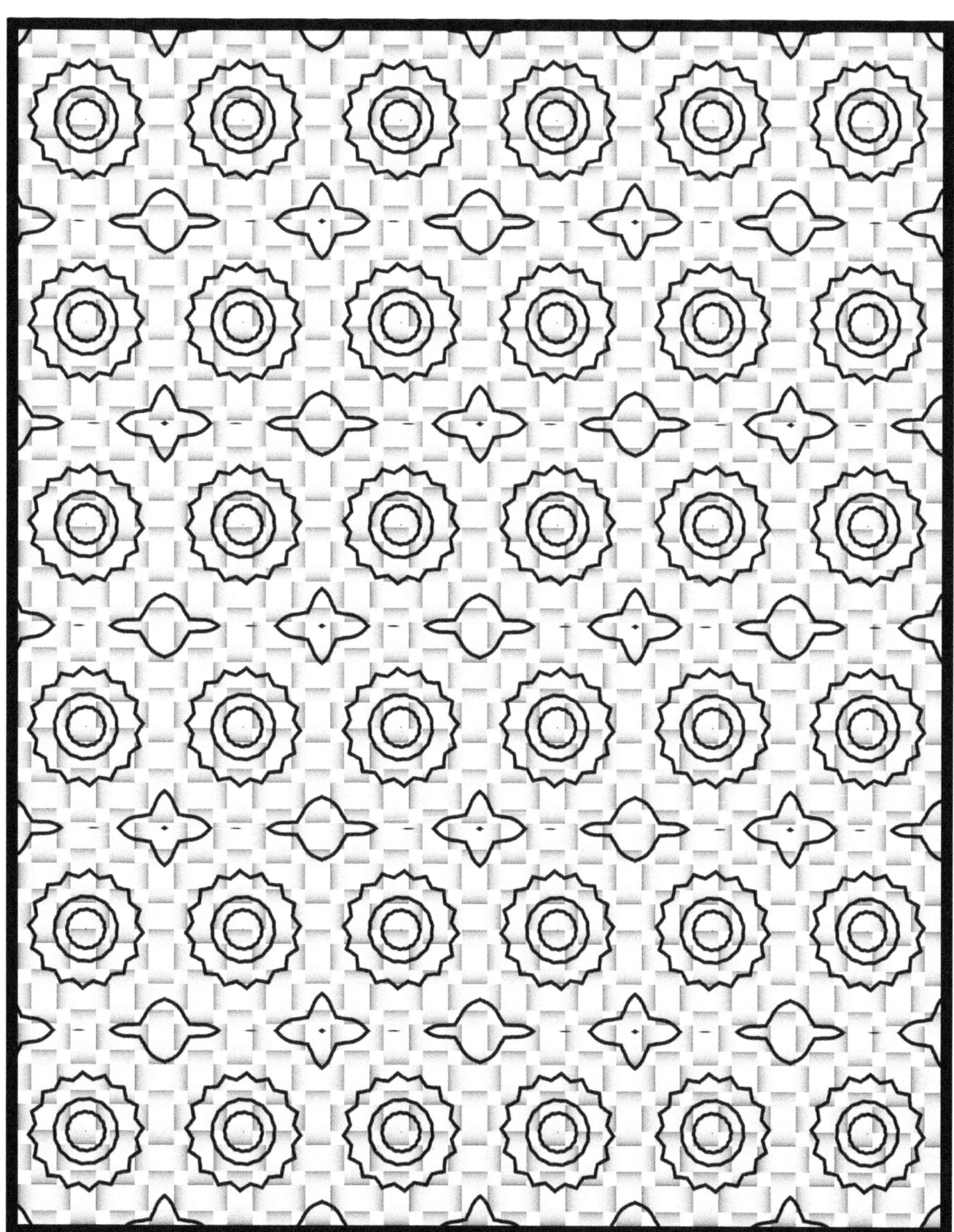

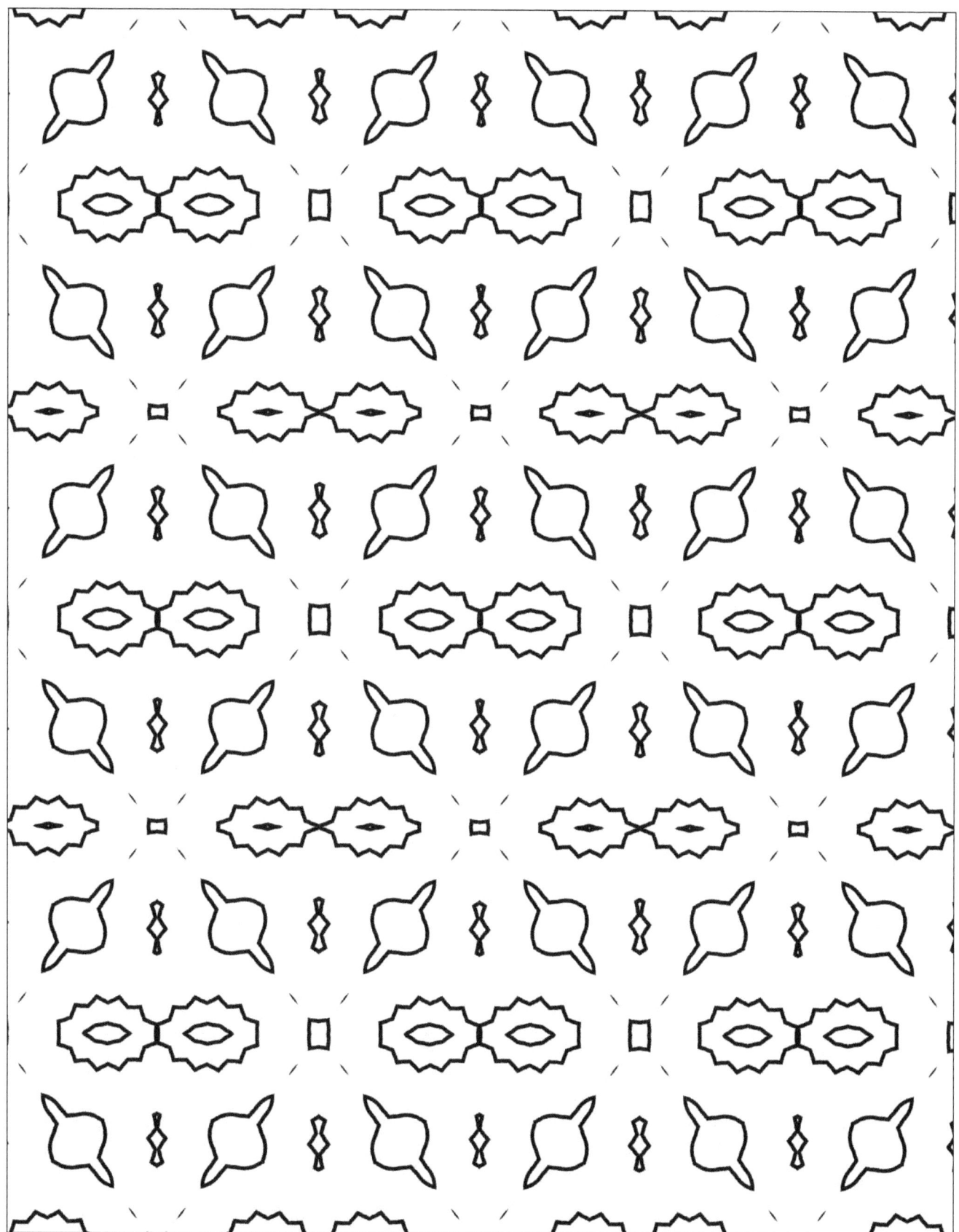

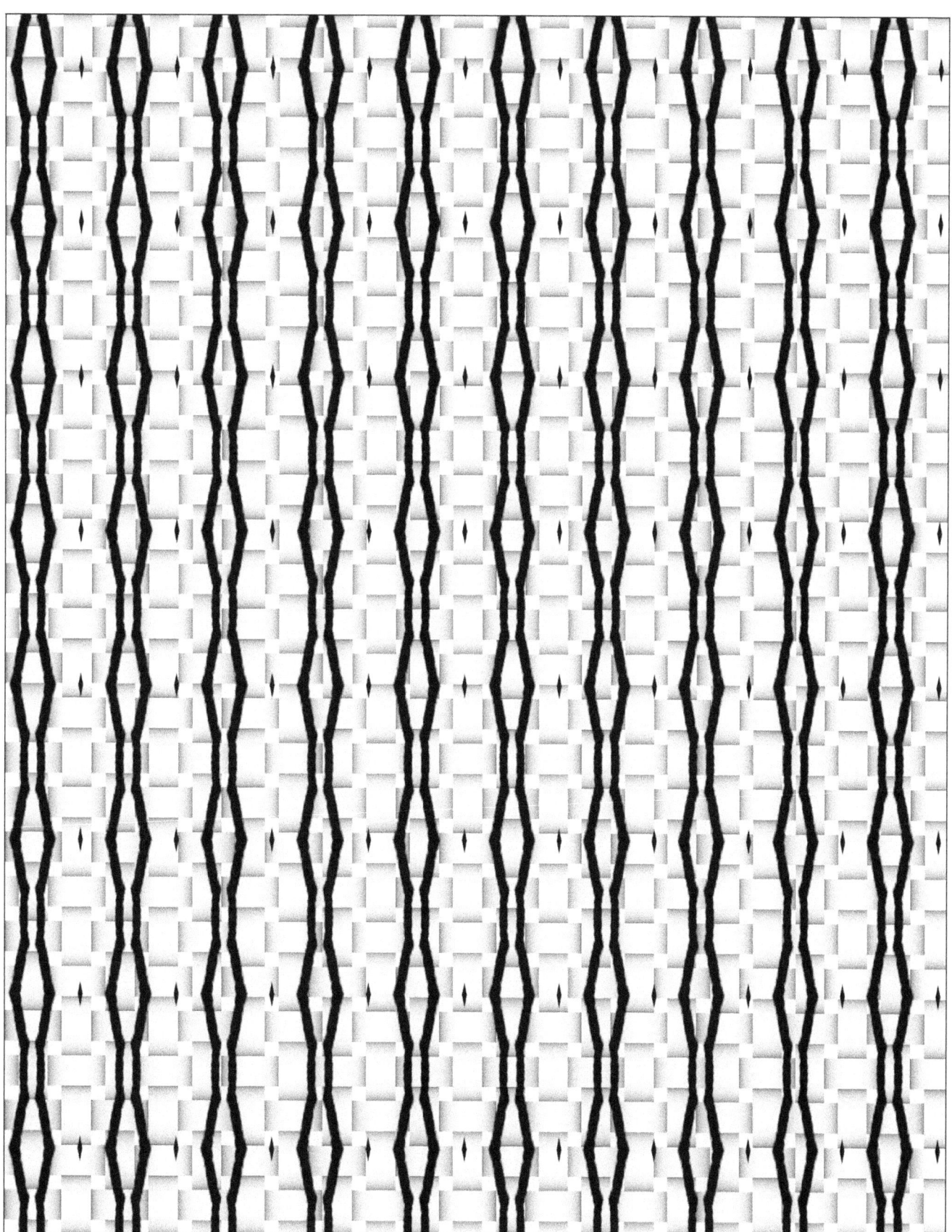

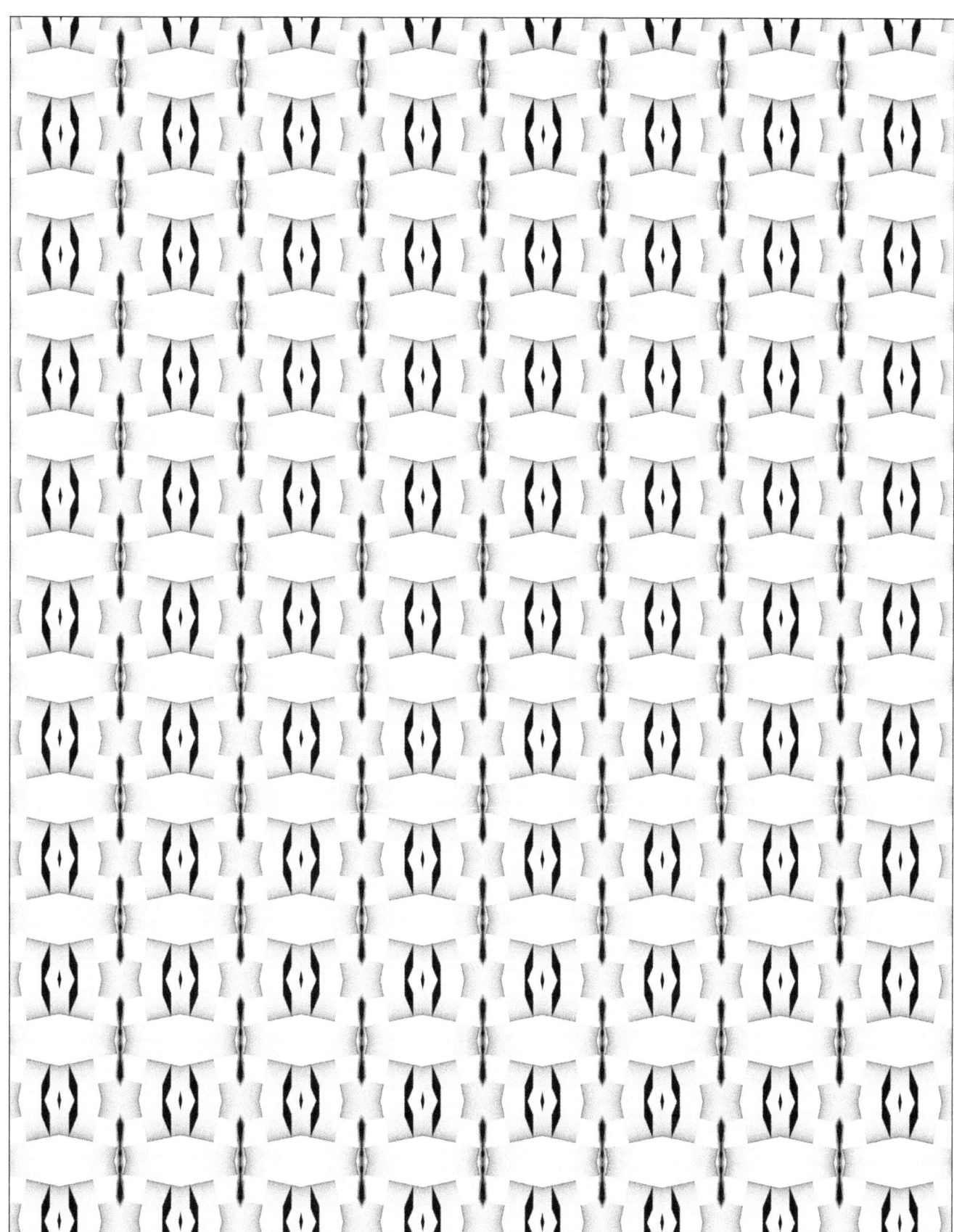

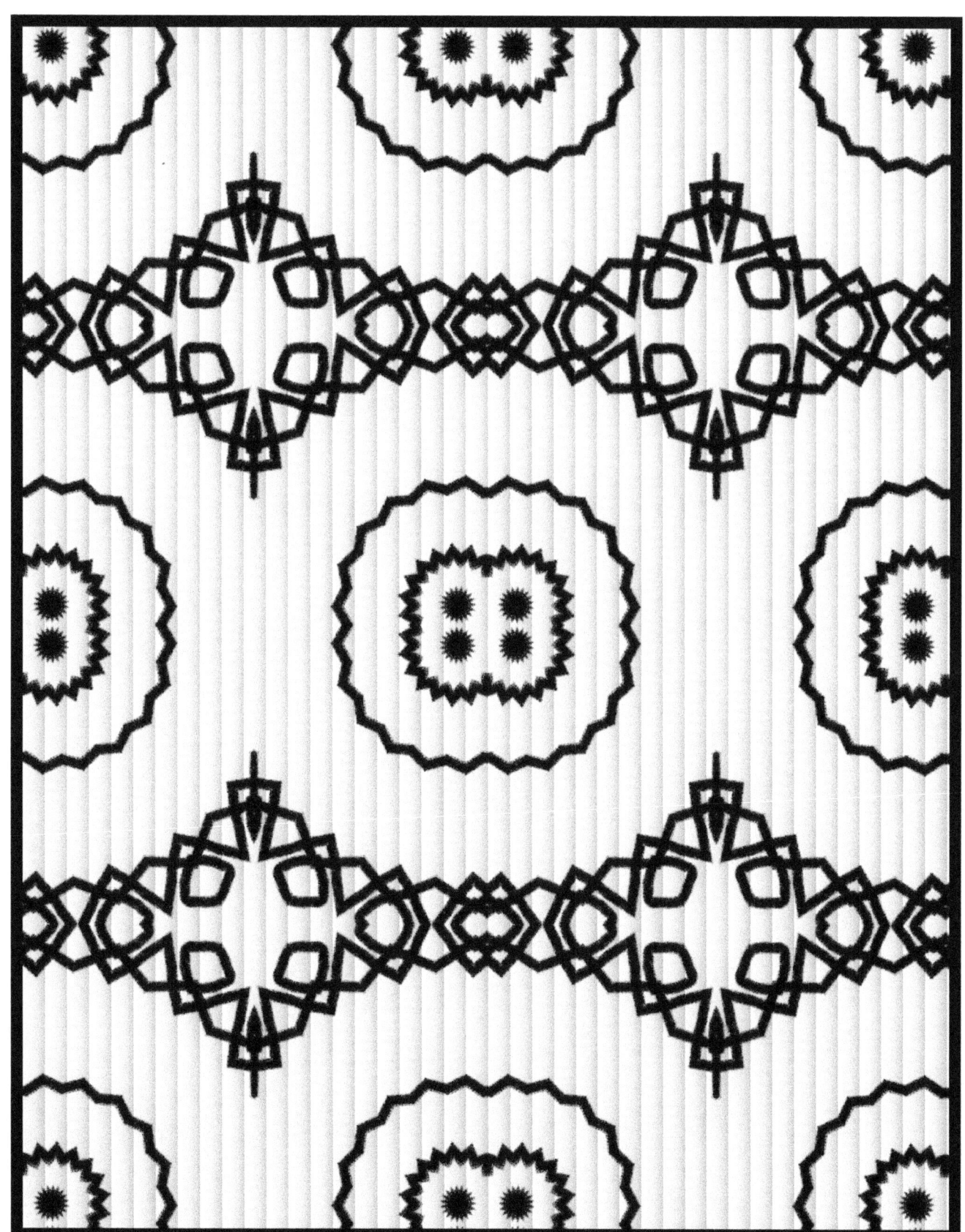

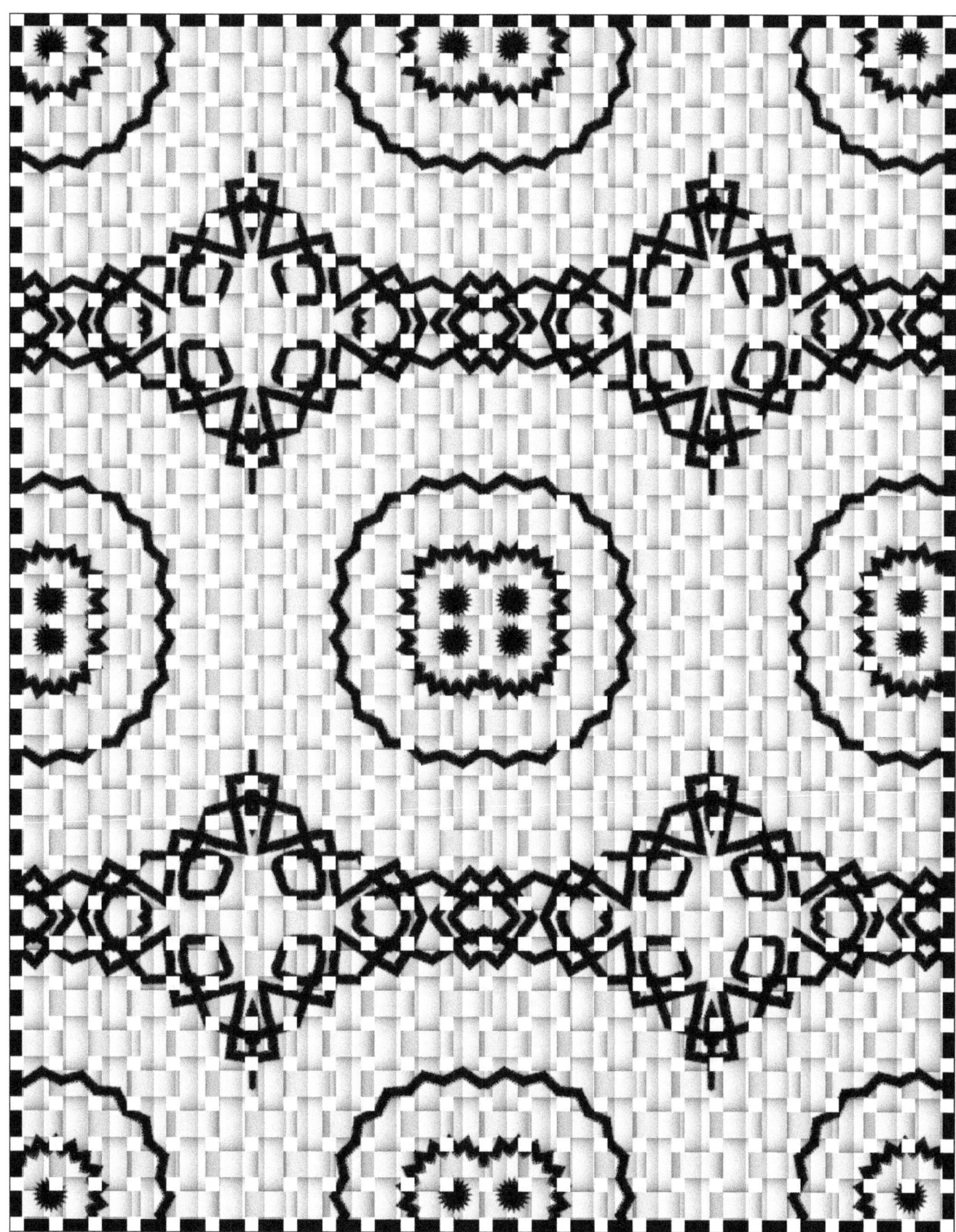

61

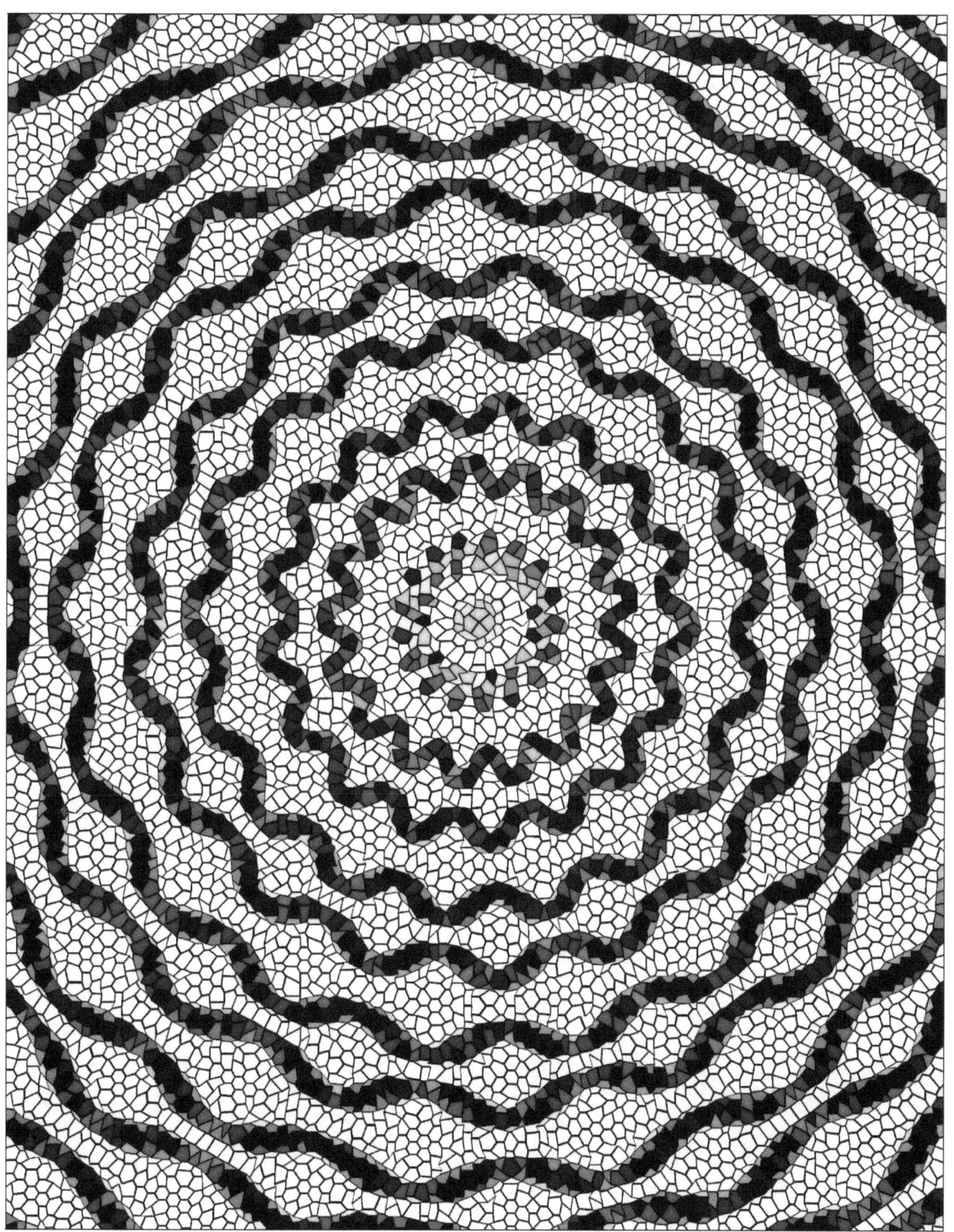

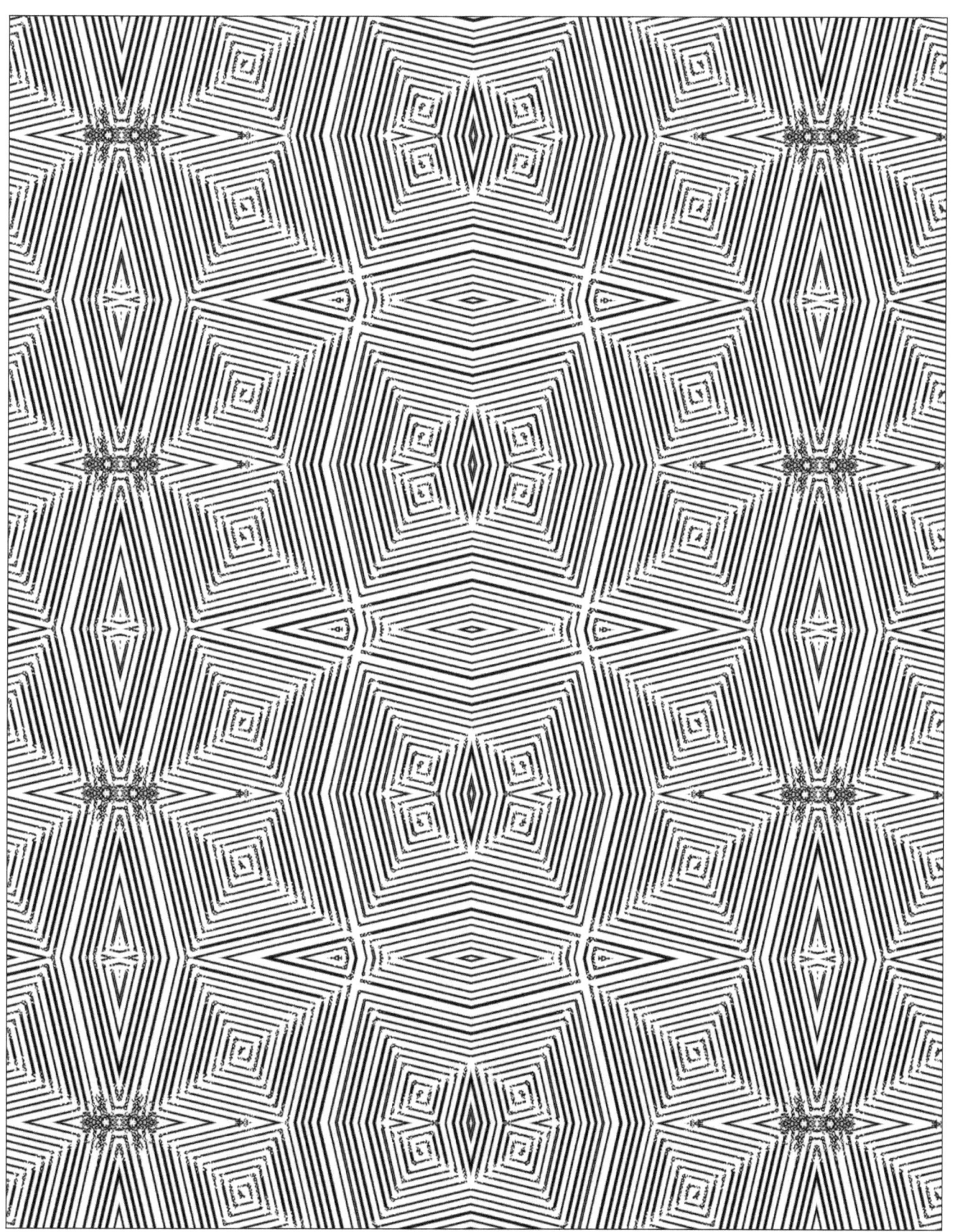

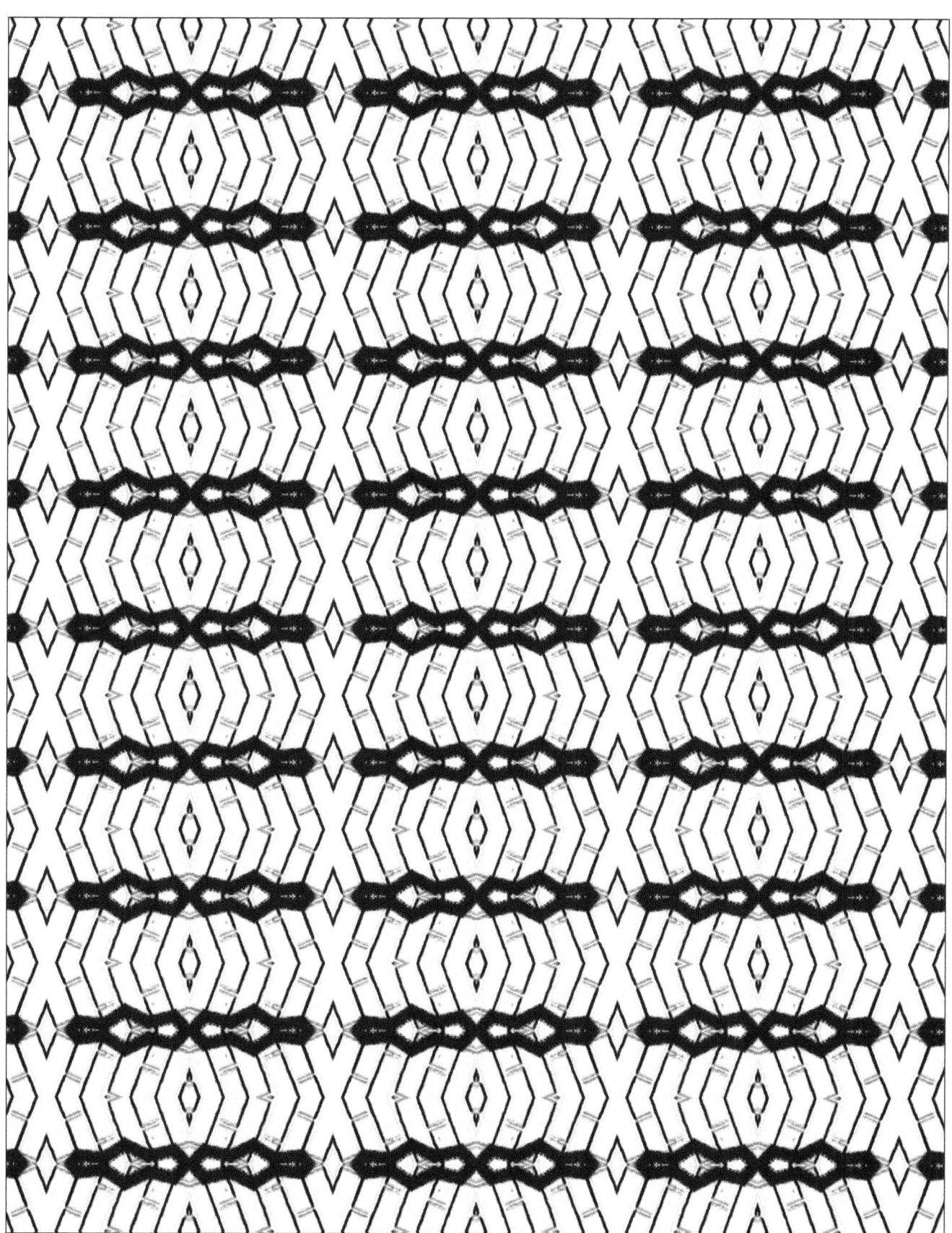

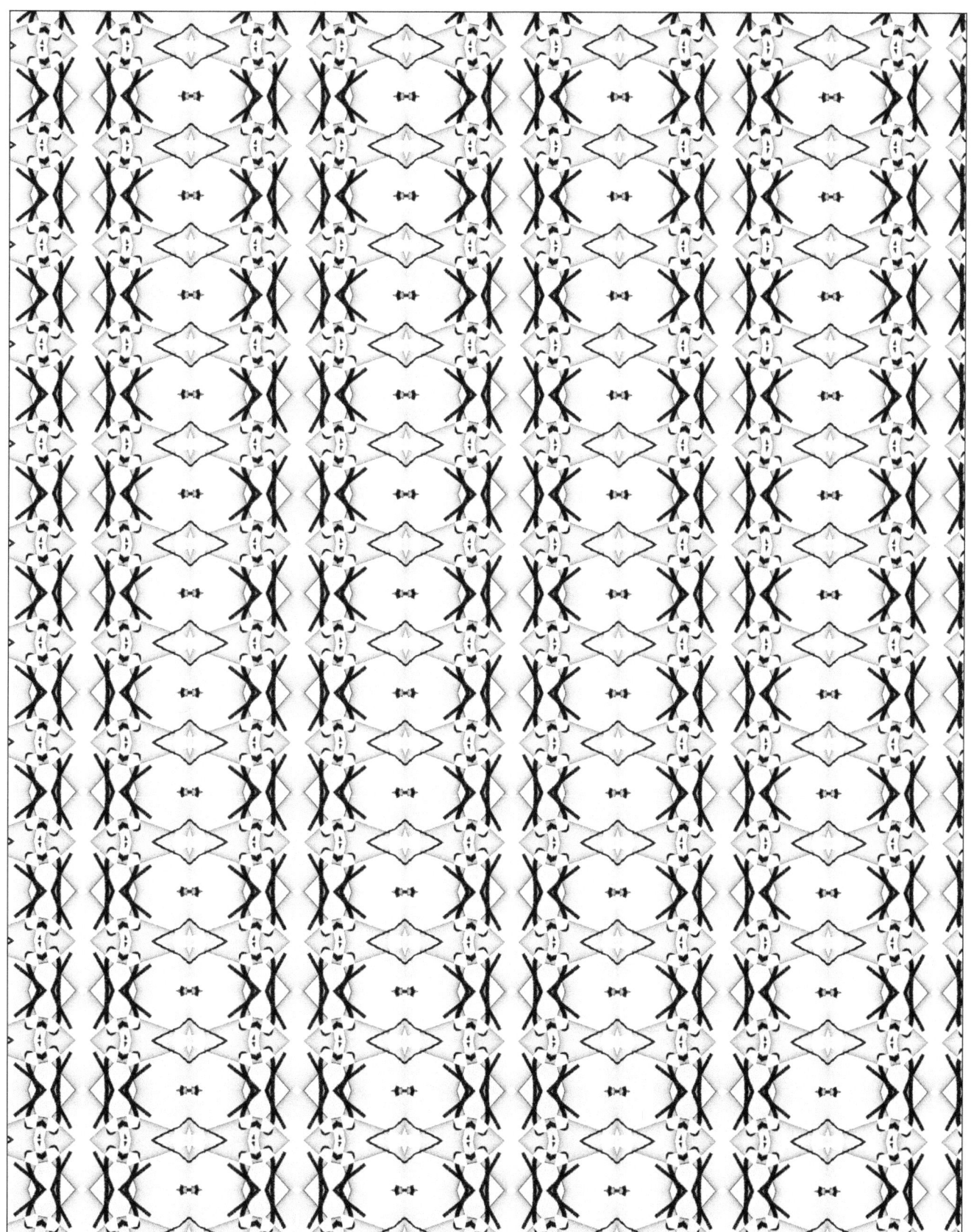

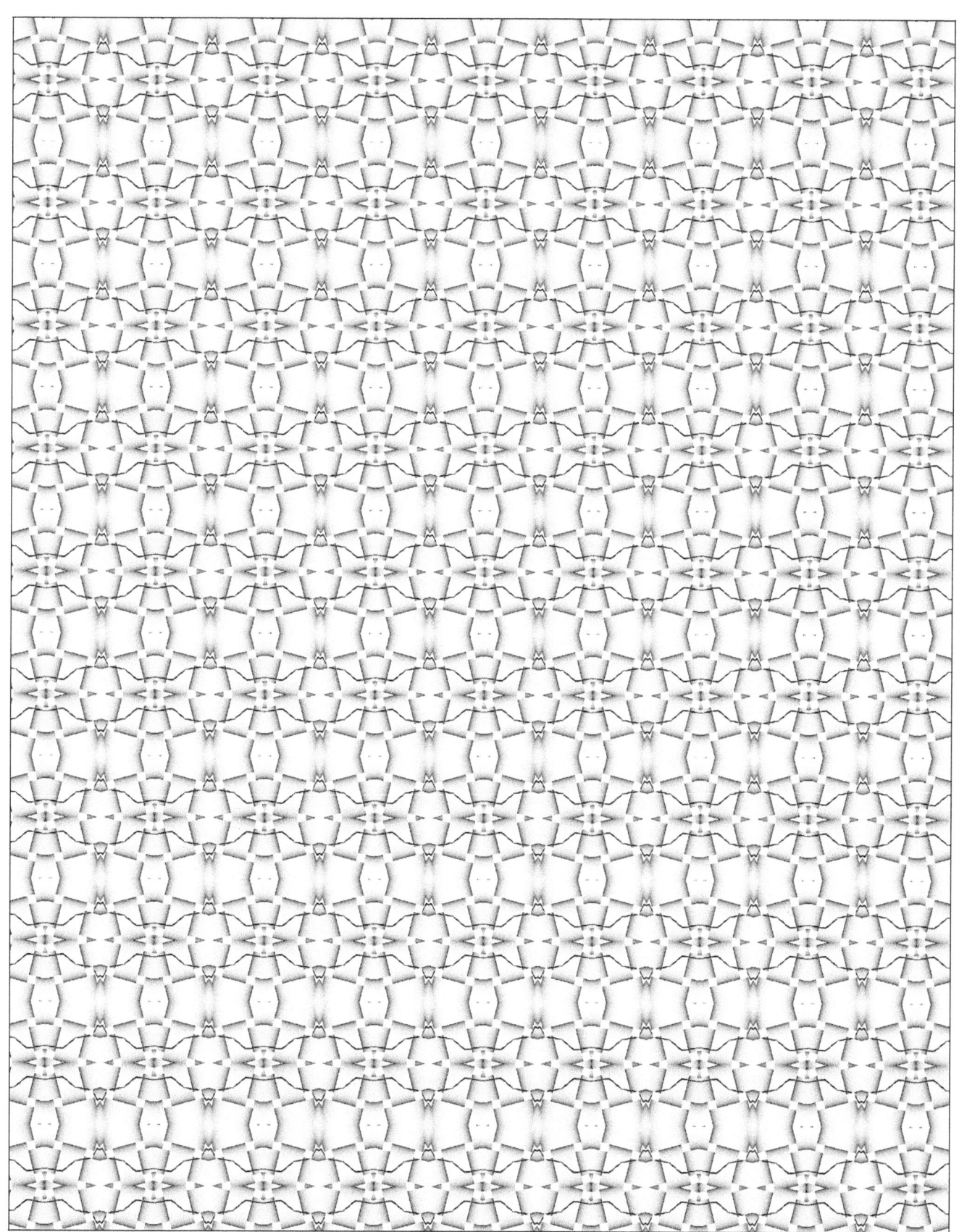

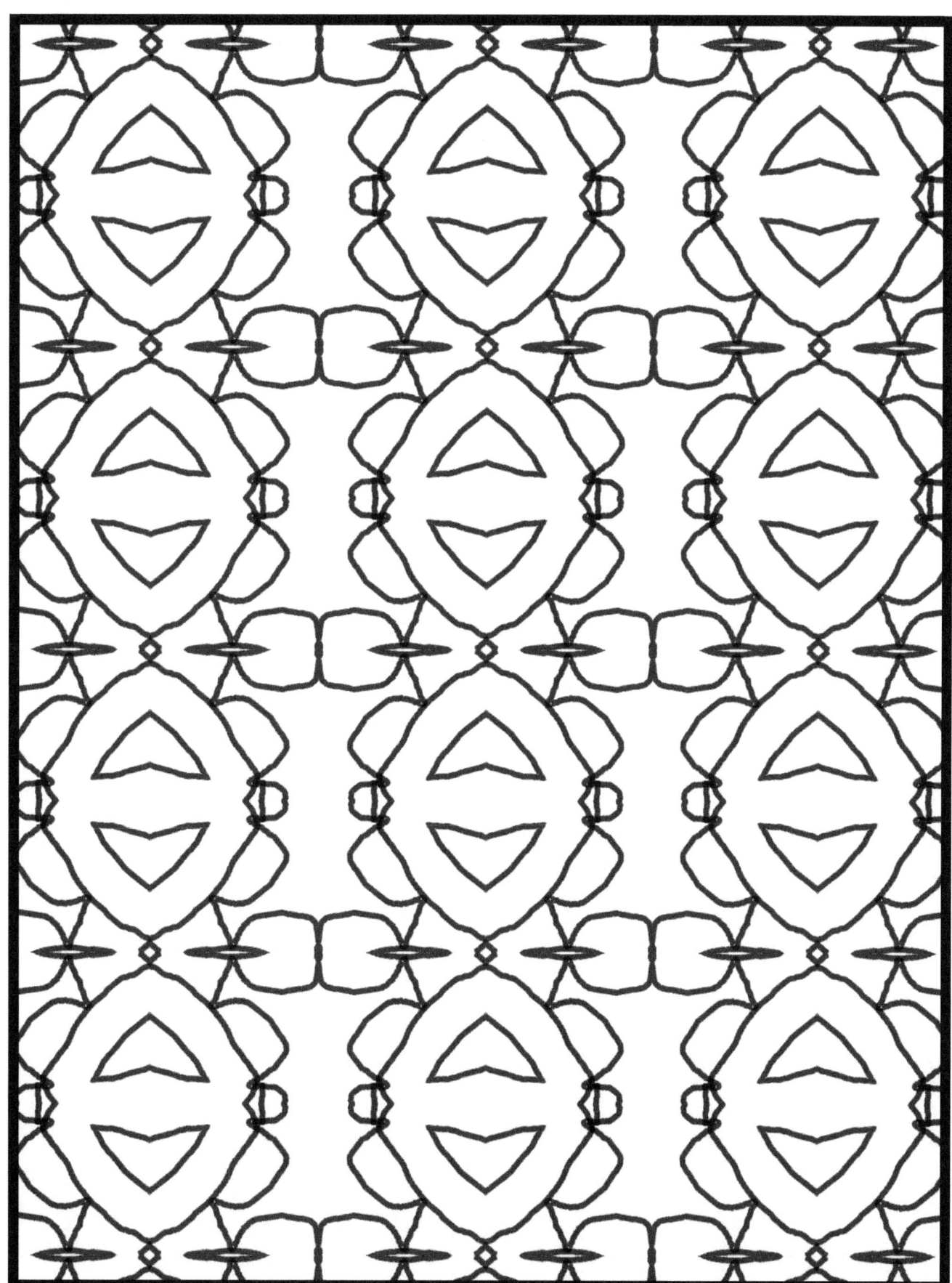

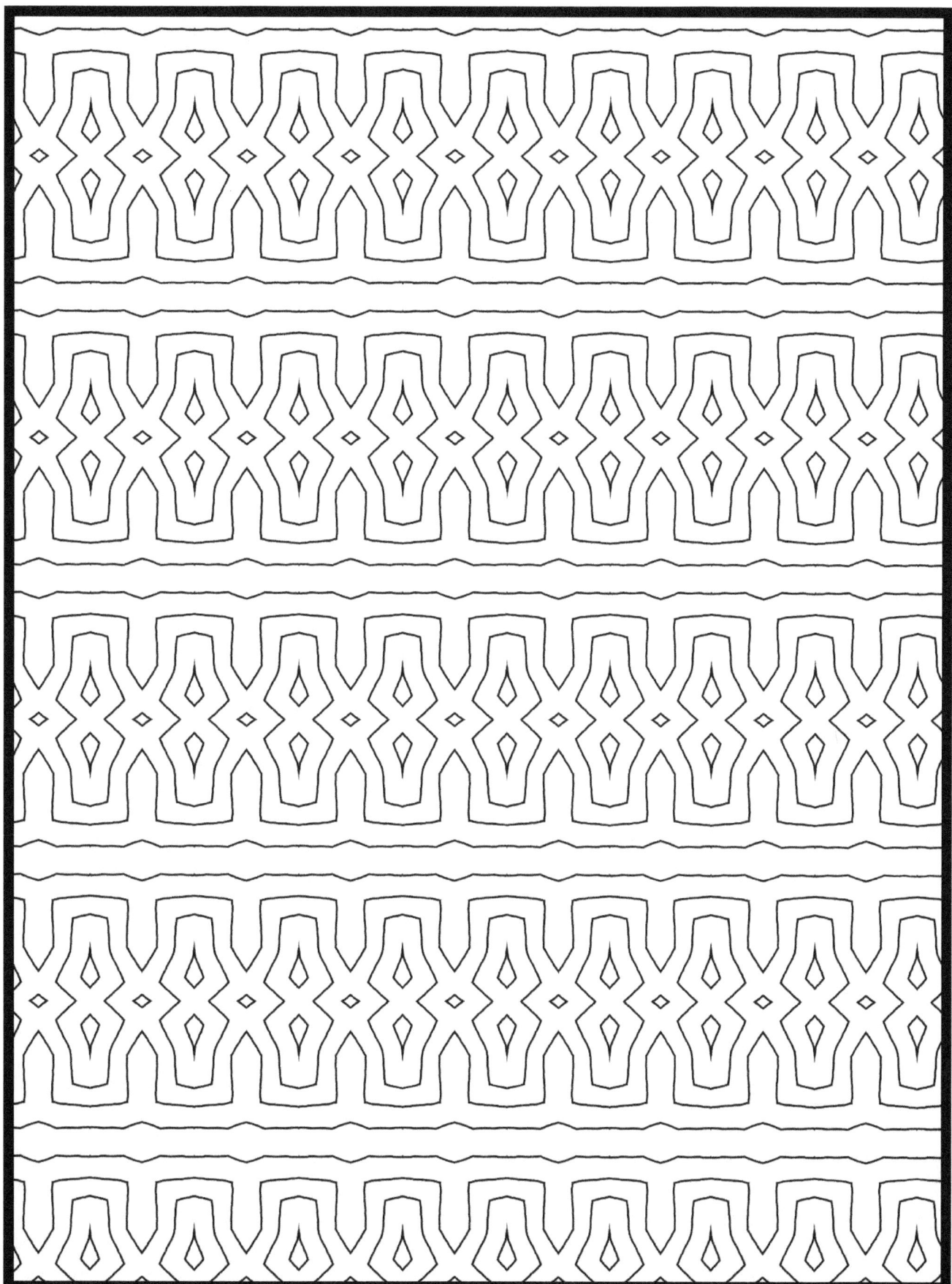

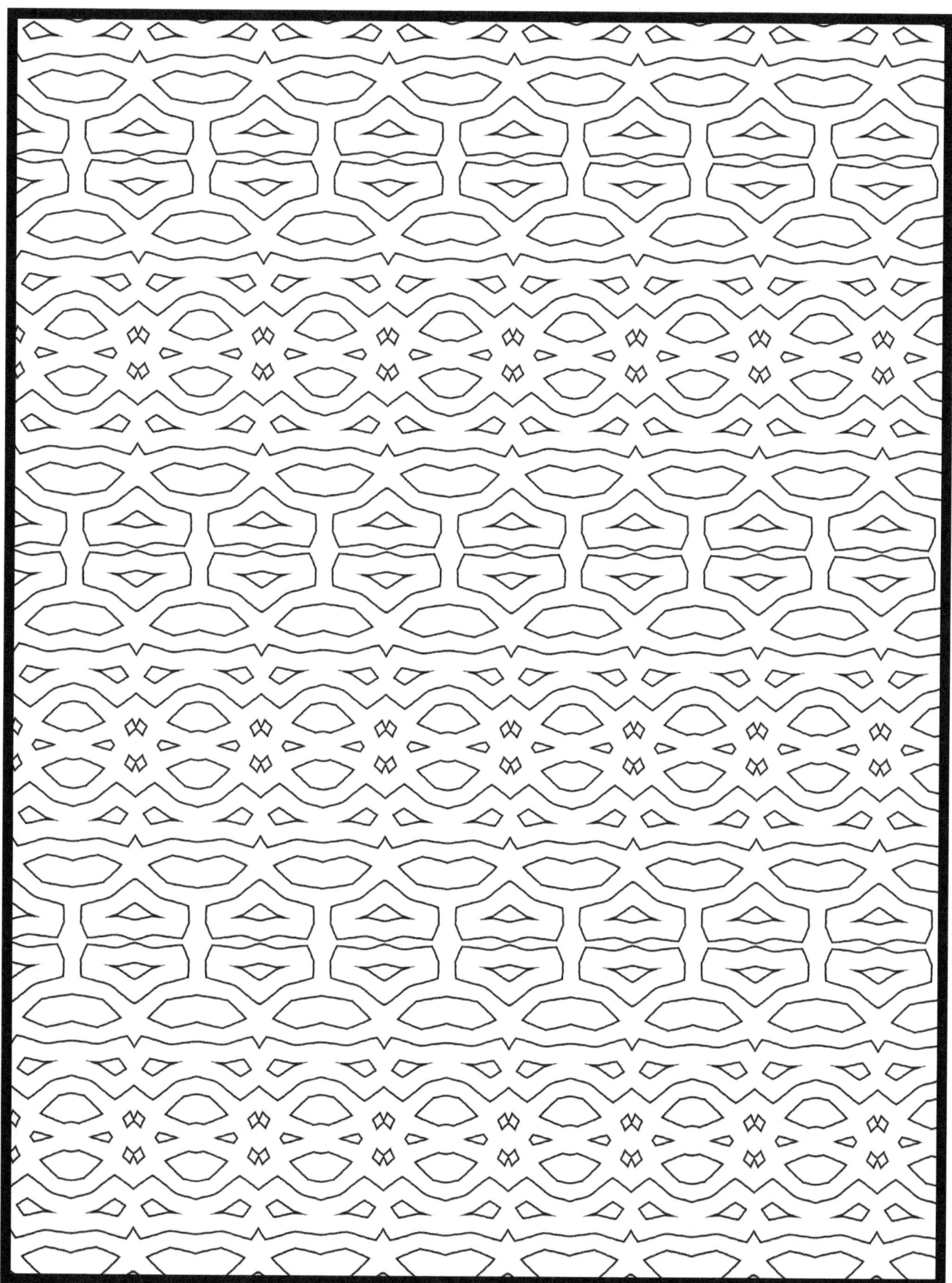

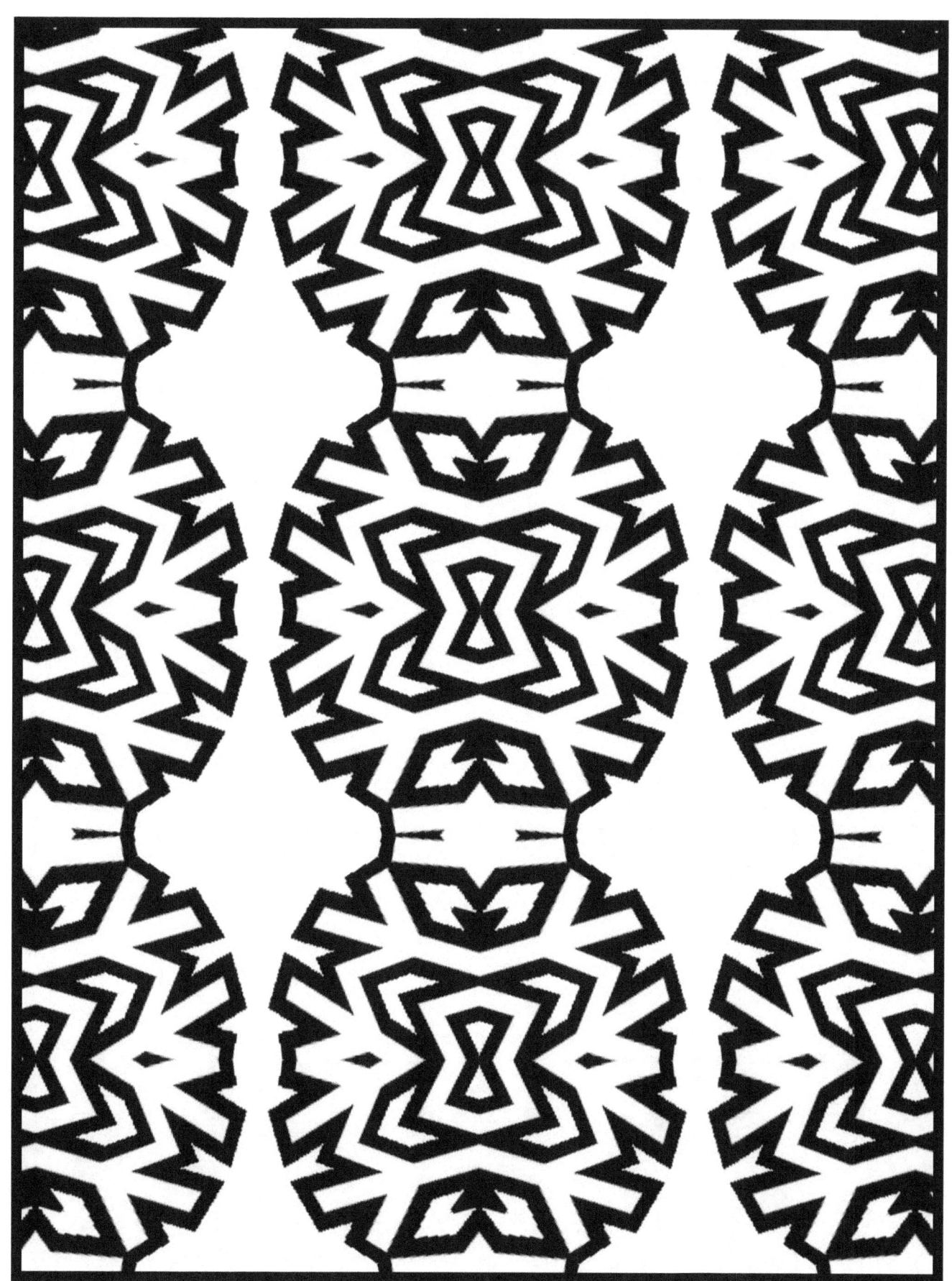

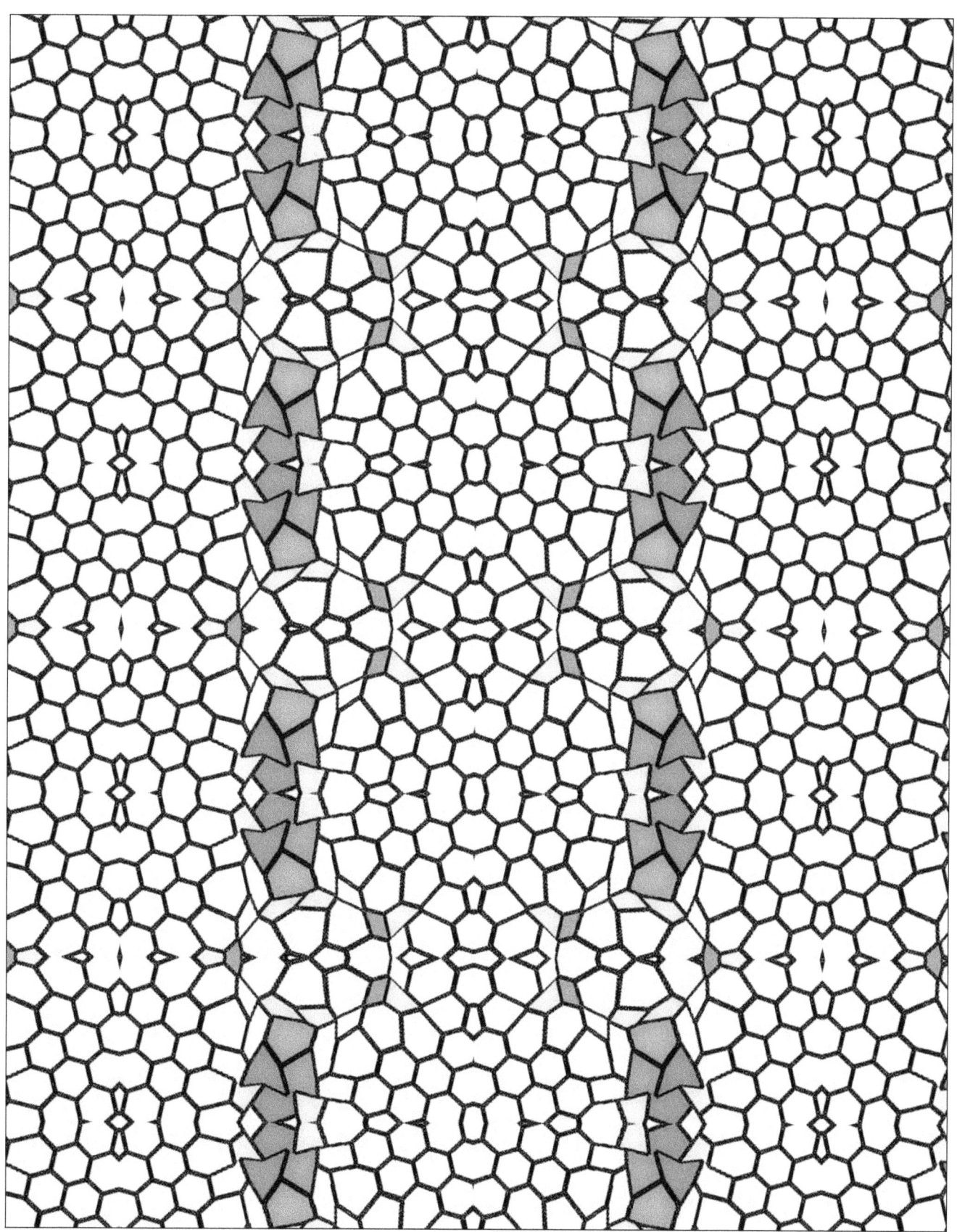

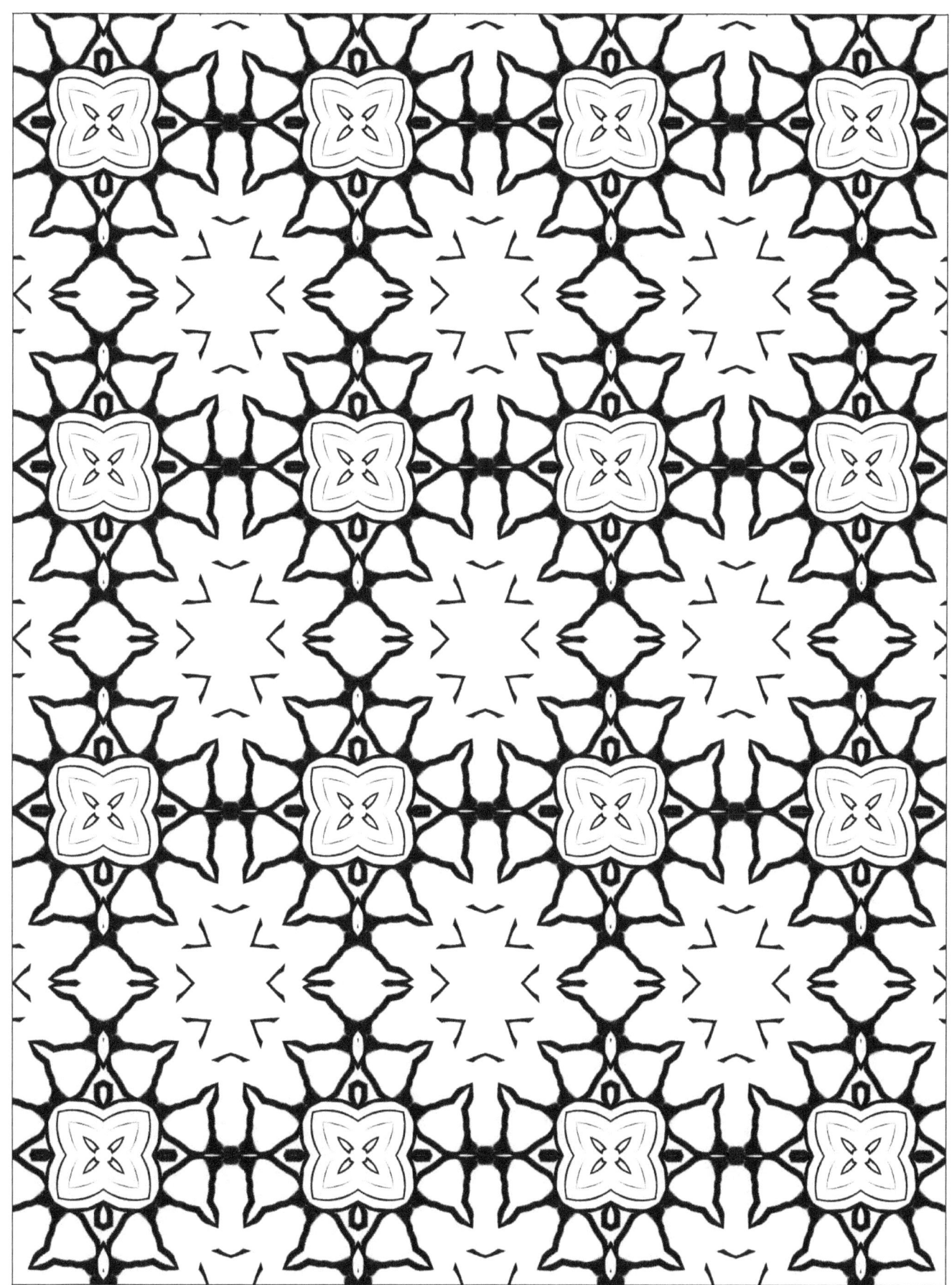

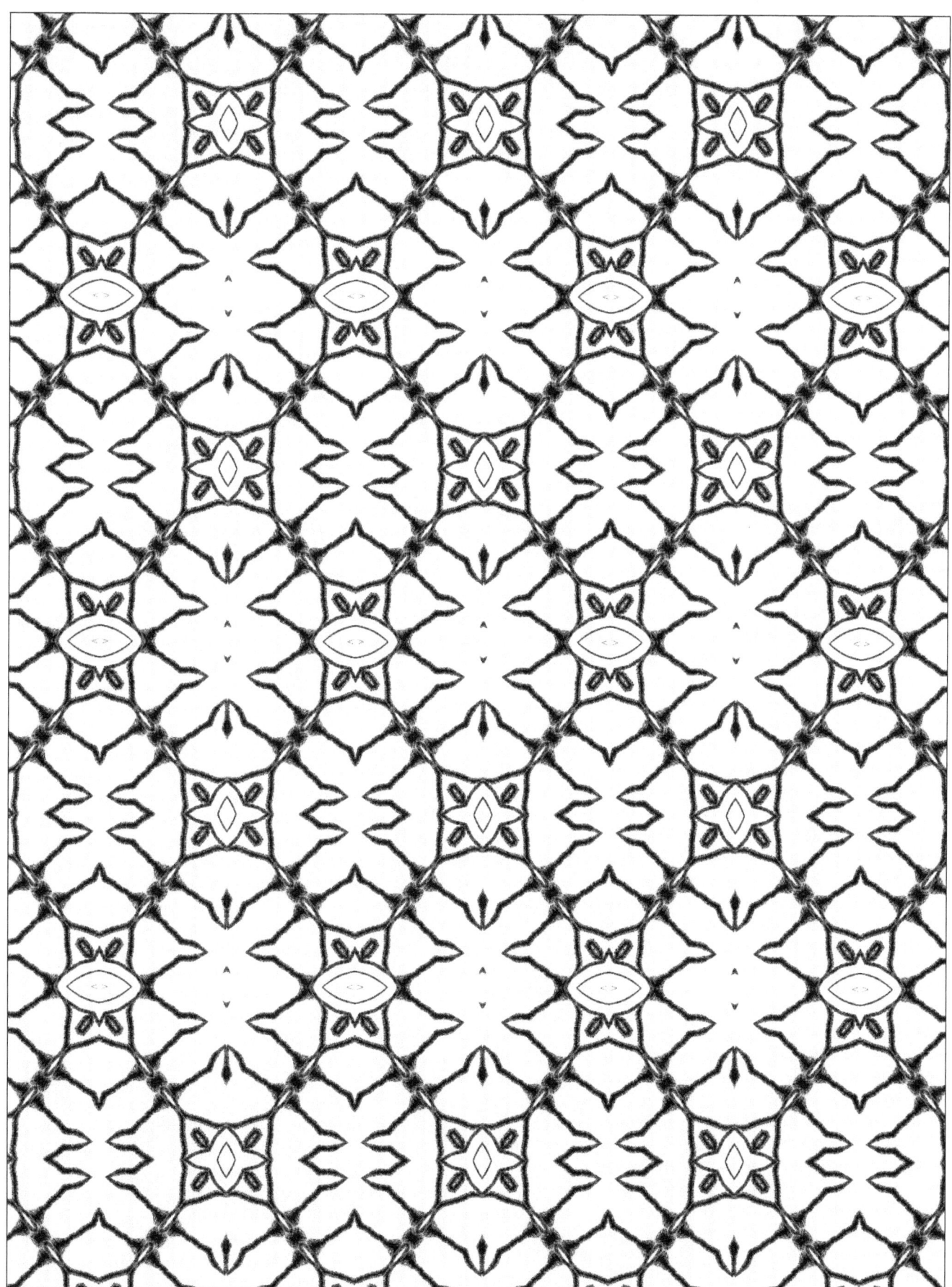

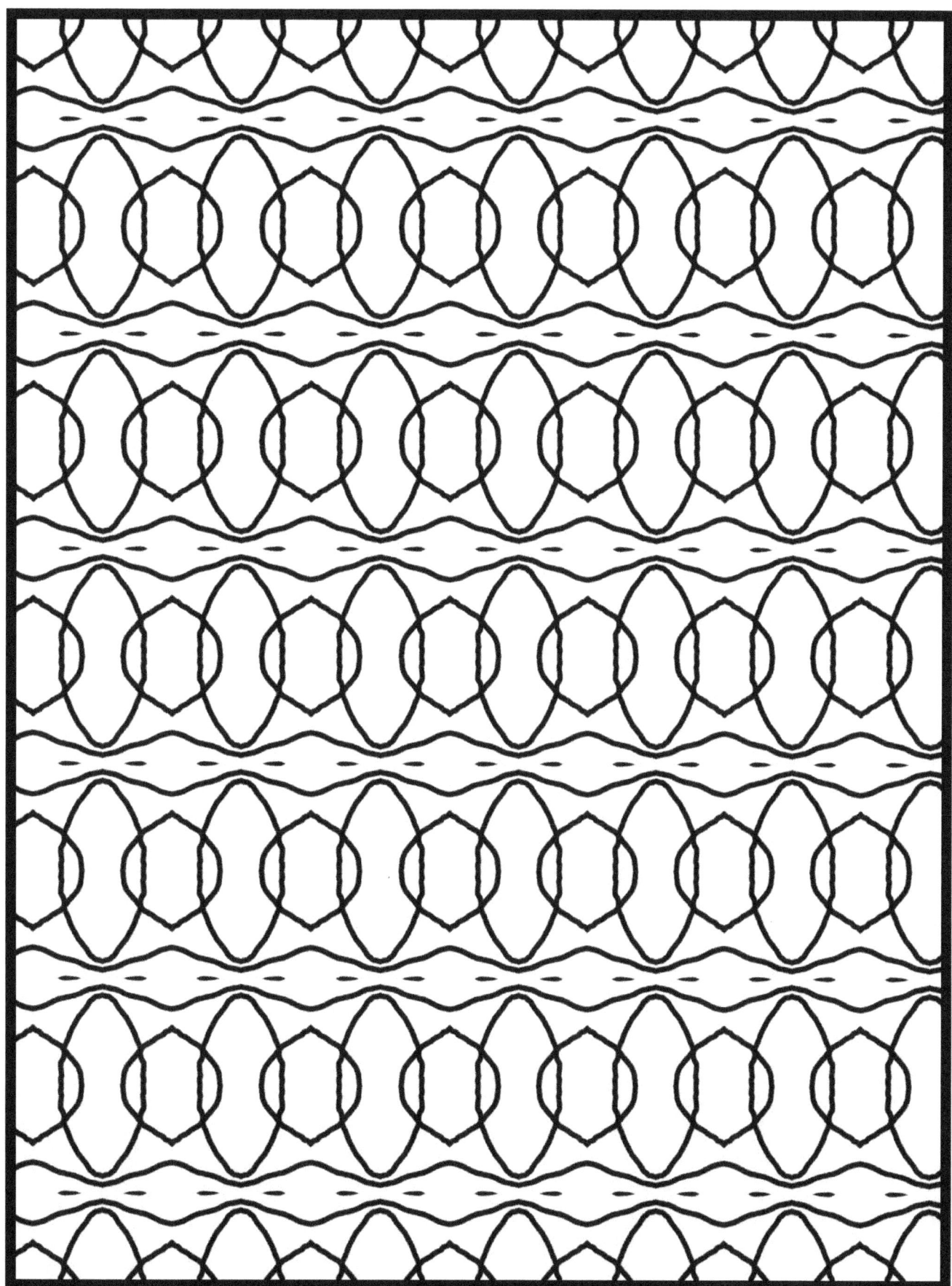

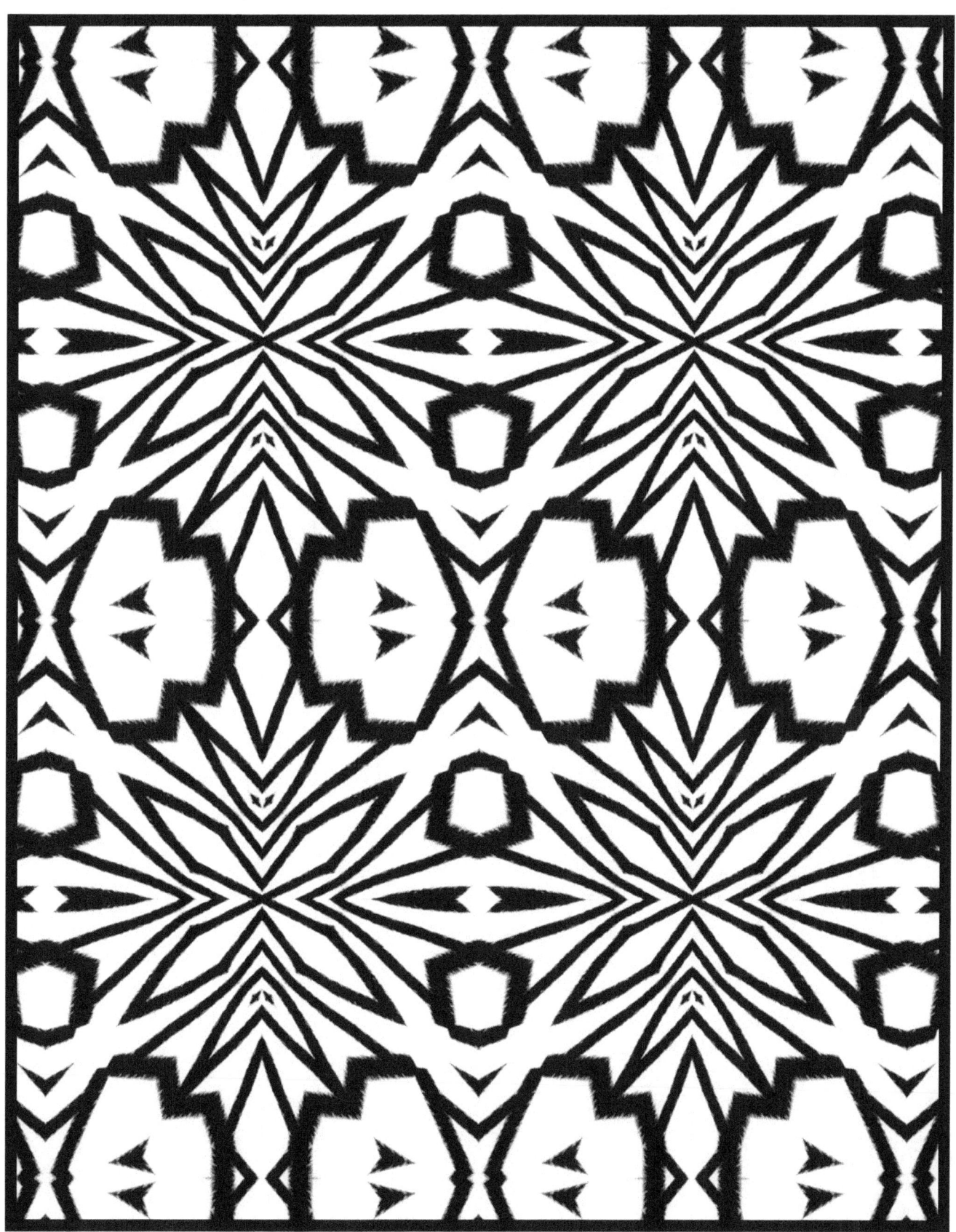

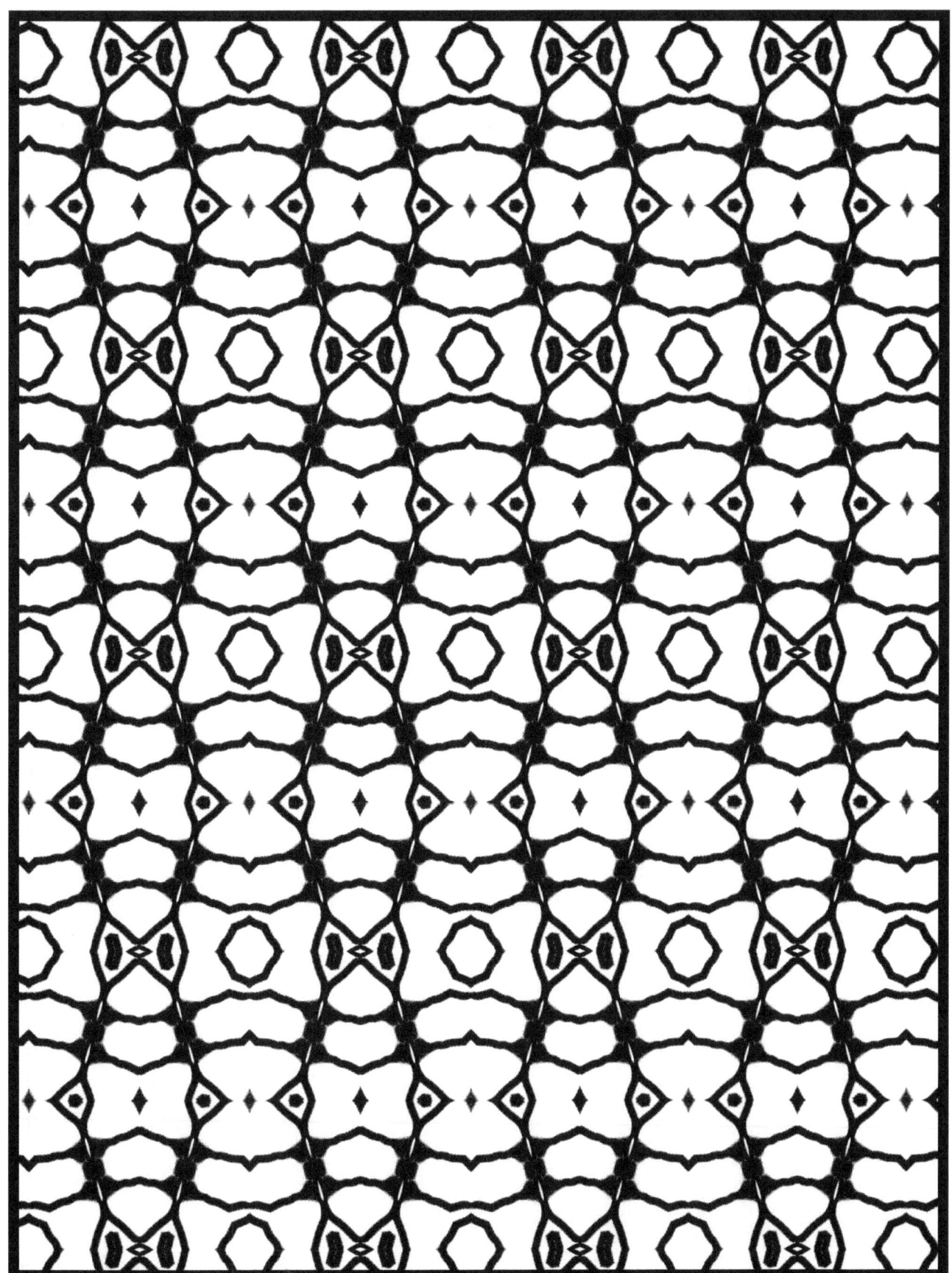

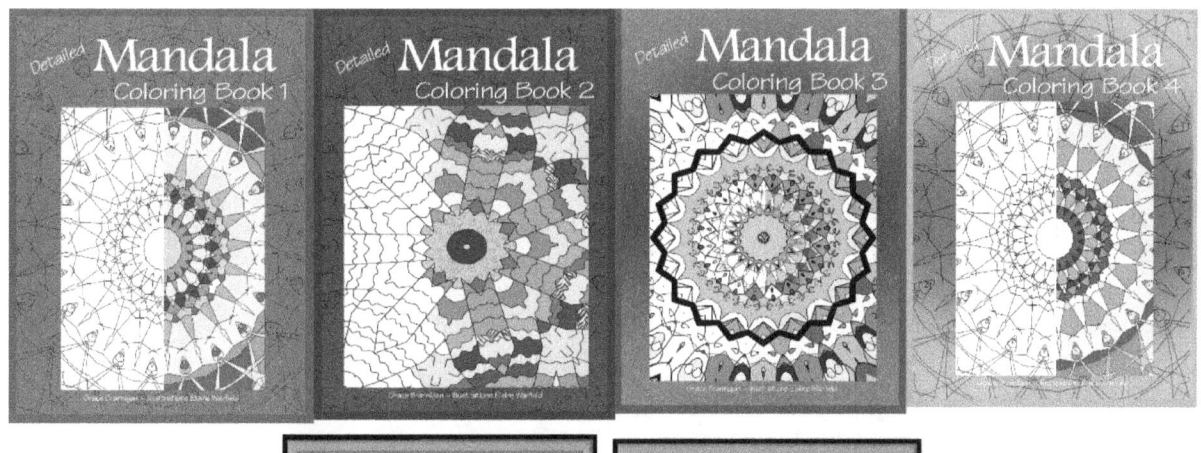

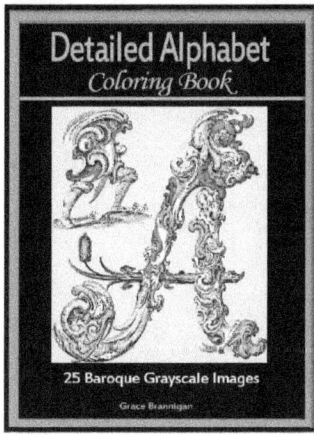 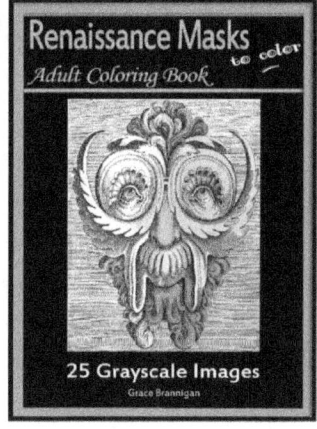

I hope you enjoyed these interesting and detailed geometric patterns to color. Thank you for purchasing. Please go back to where you bought this book and leave feedback. It really helps the authors and potential buyers. Check out my website for other coloring books!

http://www.ColoringBooksForAdults.info